Mark Twain
and the
Backwoods Angel

MARK TWAIN AND THE BACKWOODS ANGEL

The Matter of Innocence in the Works of Samuel L. Clemens

WILLIAM C. SPENGEMANN

The Kent State University Press

KENT STUDIES IN ENGLISH
General Editor, Howard P. Vincent

I. *Essays on Determinism in American Literature*
Edited by Sydney J. Krause

II. *The Computer and Literary Style*
Edited by Jacob Leed

III. *Bartleby, The Scrivener: The Melville Annual*
Edited by Howard P. Vincent

IV. *Mark Twain and the Backwoods Angel*
By William C. Spengemann

The selections from *Roughing It, A Connecticut Yankee in King Arthur's Court,* and *Personal Recollections of Joan of Arc* by Mark Twain are reprinted by courtesy of Harper and Row, Publishers. In addition, acknowledgment is made for the selection from *The Mysterious Stranger and Other Stories,* Copyright 1916 by Harper and Brothers; renewed Copyright 1944 by Clara Clemens Gabrilowitsch, by permission of Harper and Row, Publishers.

The poem from *The Complete Poems of Emily Dickinson,* edited by Thomas H. Johnson, is reprinted by permission of Little, Brown and Company, Copyright 1914 and 1942 by Martha Dickinson Bianchi, and by permission of the publishers and The Trustees of Amherst College: The Belknap Press of Harvard University Press, Copyright 1951 and 1955 by The President and Fellows of Harvard College.

Quotations from the Mark Twain–William Dean Howells correspondence are reprinted by permission of Thomas G. Chamberlain, President, the Mark Twain Company.

For Phyl

Contents

Introduction ix

1. The Backwoodsman and the Pilgrim 1
   The Genesis of the Innocent Hero

2. The Greenhorn and the Captain 15
   Roughing It and
   "Captain Stormfield's Visit to Heaven"

3. The Fallen Woman and the Bad Boy 31
   The Gilded Age and *Tom Sawyer*

4. The Cub, the Changeling and the Recruit 48
   "Old Times on the Mississippi,"
   The Prince and the Pauper and
   "A Campaign That Failed"

5. The Backwoods Angel 61
   Adventures of Huckleberry Finn

6. The Yankee Pirate 84
   A Connecticut Yankee in King Arthur's Court

7. The Saint 105
   Joan of Arc

8. The Angel 120
   The Mysterious Stranger

Notes to the Text 135

Index 143

Eden is that old-fashioned House
We dwell in every day
Without suspecting our abode
Until we drive away

How fair on looking back, the Day
We sauntered from the Door—
Unconscious our returning,
But discover it no more.

EMILY DICKINSON

Introduction

THIS BOOK IS an examination of Mark Twain's use of the matter of innocence from his earliest writings to the anxious outpourings of his latest phase. It suggests that for him the idea of American innocence amounted to a faith which he could neither abjure nor accept uncritically and that the major strain of his work documents this moral dilemma. As the reader proceeds from the work of Clemens' apprentice years, through *Huckleberry Finn,* to the testaments of pessimism written in his old age, he is struck by evidence of a mind clinging desperately to traditional values in an age which increasingly denied their validity. The struggle is moving and monumental, not only because it occurs in a man whom we cannot help but love, but because it mirrors in that especially sensitive and articulate being the turmoil of his whole age, and of ours.

The idea of innocence, of essential human goodness, has teased the Western intellect with its possibilities, its improbabilities, its potentialities, and its latent heresies, as long as there has been a set of attitudes that can be considered, in any sense, Western. The notion has appeared in so many guises, surrounded by so many conditions and qualifications, and applied to so many different situations, that it is almost impossible to generalize very intelligently about it without leaving out as many characteristics as we may mention. But, out of all the complex details which enrich the history of this compelling idea, one clear pattern does emerge, one intellectual trend so significant that it makes all subtler facts appear as momentary fluctuations on a perfect curve. It is, simply, that while innocence may have been a subject of speculation and surmise for two thousand years in Europe, in America it became a basis for belief and action. While its possibilities presented themselves to philosophers and artists in the Old World, the same possibilities took the shape of tacit assumptions in the cultural life of millions of Americans.

In America the idea of innocence entails the belief that the individual will, operating in a naturally permissive environment, can dictate right action without recourse either to institutional dogma or to educated reason. Like the definitive religious man, the hero of the American myth of innocence identifies himself in relation to a constant spiritual force. This conviction he feels about his identity gives him both a large measure of security and, often, extreme confidence in the efficacy of his will. Intuitively sure of his rightness, of his affinity with God in Nature, the innocent hero usually confronts the world with infinite good will and expects it to deal with him in the same spirit. He generally behaves as if a pure heart were the source of unconquerable strength, and he seldom recognizes any force in the world which he cannot identify, isolate, and conquer.

The myth itself is an intricate blend of at least four ingredients: the ancient European dream of the lost paradise to be regained; the spirit of American Calvinism, both in its aristocratic, New England cast and in the more democratic form which grew out of the Great Awakening; the idealistic political theories of the Enlightenment and of European Romanticism, with their perfectionist visions and their faith in the nobility of free and responsible men; and the pioneer experience itself, which gave to originally European ideas their uniquely American flavor by attaching them to the landscape of the New World. Guided by the self-image and the world view which these components created, Americans proceeded to build a new civilization in the wilderness; but the civilization was strangely out of keeping with the expectations which loosed the energy required in the building.

Nineteenth-century American history seems to describe an increasing irreconcilability between the expectations and the facts of American life. Understandably enough, it was in this period that our writers devoted themselves to the task of defining and testing the mythology upon which so much of our national identity continues to rest. Hawthorne, Melville, and Emily Dickinson went so far in their respective examinations of American belief as to suggest that not only is innocence an insufficient bulwark against corruption, but that the pursuit of innocence is itself corrupting. Clemens never went so far, but his work is no less an indictment of American faith for all of his apparent unwillingness to abandon the beliefs he shared with his countrymen. On the contrary, whereas the other giants of our literature drew their strength and insight from their brooding aloofness, Clemens took his from his astonishing closeness to the beliefs of his countrymen. Anyone who reads his work in this light cannot help but be struck by the extent to which popular attitudes directed his fiction.

As Clemens presents it, the myth of American innocence entails three distinguishable but obviously related problems. First, and most important for Clemens, is the moral drama which the myth implies. In this drama, the innocent hero, who behaves with an instinctive sense of rightness, confronts characters and situations which represent the forces of evil and then pursues a course of action which leads, first, to recognition, then to either evasion by the innocent, to total defeat of one of the contestants, or to a compromise between them.

This moral conflict is, at the same time, a political battle, since the virtuous hero is self-sufficient and, although naturally compassionate, highly individualistic; and since his evil adversaries represent the social sins of uniformity, sham, and repression of virtuous instinct. Like his countrymen, of his time and ours, Clemens equated the problems of personal morality with political identity. Depending on their political persuasion, Americans have habitually equated individuality and social uniformity, respectively, with either good or evil. And since Clemens, despite some reversals of opinion which caused him no end of personal disquietude, worked out of the republican ideal of the free individual, he generally associated the apostle of the self-determined spirit with goodness and the minions of civilized institutions with evil. Unfortunately, however, he not only equated politics and morality, he confused them. Influenced by his Calvinist training, he denied the possibility of compromise between the forces of good and evil. As a result, he saw no possible compromise between the individual and society. Allegorizing his experience in the manner of his Calvinist forebears, he saw the war between the individual and society as a symbol of the metaphysical struggle between good and evil; and following the theories of democratic Evangelism, he took the side of the individual. His strict adherence to this faith led him to inevitable disillusionment as industrialization and urbanization extended social control over nineteenth-century America.

Consequently, the second aspect of the myth which arrested Clemens' attention is the conflict between agrarian and urban, industrial values. His innocents come from the country and derive their strength from a union with unspoiled nature. In fact, even city-bred innocents, like the Greenhorn of *Roughing It,* become virtuous and compassionate as soon as they leave the artificiality and confinement of the town and enter the wide-open spaces of the country. Once again Clemens' moral judgments are tied to impossible situations, for the country was vanishing in the nineteenth century as quickly as was the absolutely free man. Equating goodness with the rapidly disappearing wilderness, Clemens set himself up for inevitable disillusionment.

The third problem which Clemens treats raises his work above the commonplace and mitigates the condition of simplemindedness which the two previous ideas seem to imply. That is, while holding tenaciously to the simplistic morality which equates the individualistic rural dweller with goodness and the socially-directed urbanite with evil, Clemens was continually examining the reliability of his faith by putting it to the imaginative test of setting, character, and action. Although he was devoted to his creed, he was too honest to accept it without trying to make it square with the facts of his experience. This tension between faith and fact engenders the conflict which makes his best work more than a mere reflection of popular sentiment and raises *Huckleberry Finn* to the level of prophecy. But even when Clemens leans desperately in the direction of his faith and falsifies the facts of his experience in order to arrive at acceptable conclusions—as in *Joan of Arc*—the works which result, sentimental as they are, testify to the anguish which many Americans felt as history scoffed at their faith in the nineteenth century.

Considered as an objectification of the American dream of innocence, the body of Clemens' work discloses a coherent development, moving from early experiments with character and situation, through various accounts of the innocent's adventures, to increasingly frantic attempts to find a setting in which the innocent can act at all. Clemens' early writings, ending with *The Innocents Abroad* in 1869, show him working out a voice, an attitude, and a set of characteristic traits for the innocent hero who appears regularly in the books which follow.

Roughing It (1872) is both the first, coherent, full-length study of the innocent, and Clemens' first account of the innocent's progress from repressive urban life to the glories of rural freedom. *The Gilded Age* (1873) marks a crisis in the development of Clemens' thought, for that novel remains his only consideration of evil experience as a source of strength and broader possibility for the innocent. In *Tom Sawyer* (1876) Clemens returns to the scenes of his boyhood in hopes of finding a situation more amenable to innocence. But this novel, too, failed for him, largely because his intentions in writing it conflicted with his interest in his hero.

Huckleberry Finn (1884) arises directly out of *Tom Sawyer* and, by avoiding the errors which Clemens committed in constructing the earlier novel, offers a definitive statement on the fate of American innocence. Everyone has a pet theory about what Hemingway meant when he said that all American literature begins with this book. I prefer to think he meant that *Huckleberry Finn* explores for the first time the moral problems that arise when an individual must develop for himself an identity to carry him intact through life in a society that no longer offers him a significant and fulfilling view of himself. Whether or not Hemingway was correct in assigning this prophetic importance to *Huckleberry Finn* alone (*The Scarlet Letter* and *Moby-Dick* seem to precede in this matter), no serious American writer since Clemens has been able to ignore the issue, and we will see many more alterations in our society and in our self-image before the question is outdated.

Introduction

After *Huckleberry Finn* come the "medieval" novels, *A Connecticut Yankee in King Arthur's Court, Joan of Arc,* and *The Mysterious Stranger*. Each of these presents a picture, bleaker than its predecessor, of disillusionment about the truth and efficacy of innocence. *A Connecticut Yankee* shows the evils of which the undisciplined will is capable when the innocent invests his natural sagacity in technological progress; and like *The Mysterious Stranger* it is a work of complexity and power, despite many faults. But the major strength of all three derives from their portrayal of the despair which accompanied the defeat of the innocent by a predatory and opportunistic society. What is more, the despair was not Clemens' alone. Like the rest of his works, these later pieces crystallize in artistic form the vague apprehensions and fears of the late nineteenth and early twentieth centuries in America. Like all of his works, these later books bespeak Clemens' closeness to the intellectual history of his time. But more important, they illustrate Clemens' role as a seer, a "maker," who captured the aspirations and failures of his age and turned them into art.

Because in this book I examine what strikes me as a particularly solemn idea, I may seem to the reader to ignore Mark Twain's great gift for comedy, and so leave a significant part of his genius out of account. Perhaps unfortunately, his humor lies often outside my central concerns. Outlining his own theory of composition, Clemens once said, "*Any* lecture of mine ought to be a running narrative-plank, with square holes in it, six inches apart, all the length of it, and then in my mental shops I ought to have plugs (half marked 'serious' and the other marked 'humorous') to select from and jam into these holes according to the temper of the audience." What we see as funny in his writing generally appears as one or another of these plugs—Huck's arguments with Jim, the Greenhorn's observations on sagebrush in *Roughing It,* and Hank Morgan's tormenting suit of armor in *A Connecticut Yankee*. But the plank itself, the framework which holds and, when Clemens is at his best, makes the plugs part of its smooth surface, represents Clemens' most fundamental perceptions about human nature. The purpose of this book is to show that, however many different plugs he put into it, the plank remains significantly unchanged from *The Innocents Abroad* to *The*

Mysterious Stranger. The question of innocence prevails throughout. Perhaps the most significant thing to be said about Clemens' humor, is that he took comic materials which were *only* humorous in other hands and made them express the most complex problems of American moral history.

No reader will get far along in my argument before realizing the extent of my indebtedness to several American scholars whose works have given me a ground to stand on and survey my subject. No amount of documentation could properly indicate my indebtedness to Henry Nash Smith's two books, *Virgin Land* and *Mark Twain: The Development of a Writer;* to R. W. B. Lewis' *The American Adam;* to Charles Sanford's *The Quest for Paradise;* and to Roger B. Salomon's *Twain and the Image of History.* I have tried to indicate direct borrowings from these remarkable studies wherever they appear, but the ideas they profess have become so much a part of my thought that footnotes alone could not meet my obligation to them.

As usual, more people have contributed to this work than I can possibly name here, but some must be identified and properly thanked. I am indebted, first of all, to Thomas Moser, David Levin, and Robert Sears, all of Stanford, and to Milton Stern, of the University of Connecticut; and to Sydney Krause and Ruth Kent, of Kent State University. They all read the manuscript and offered indispensable advice on its revision. I wish to thank Professor Henry Nash Smith, of the University of California, who took time off from his own work at the Behavioral Sciences Center at Stanford, to help me get the topic within workable bounds. Thanks also to Frederick Anderson, Mr. and Mrs. Harold Ansley, Hugh Boyes, Norman Council, John Dixon, Doris Gates, James Houston, Robert Moesle, Douglas P. Walker, Ted Whittemore, and Alonzo Wiemers, each of whom contributed in important ways to my finishing this book. And to Yvor Winters I owe thanks for any signs of reverence for the human intellect which may appear in these pages. Insofar as I learned to read and write, I did so largely by studying with him.

I am grateful to the English Department of Stanford University— especially to Virgil Whitaker—and to the Woodrow Wilson Foundation, who made it financially possible for me to work uninterrupted on portions of this book. The Research Foundation of the University of Connecticut enabled me to pay for professional secretarial help.

And finally, I want to do in print something that I will also try to find less academic ways of doing: thank my wife for the long hours she spent tending the manuscript and its irascible writer.

W. C. S.

Storrs, Connecticut
October 1966

1.

The Backwoodsman and the Pilgrim

THE GENESIS OF
THE INNOCENT HERO

I**N EACH OF** Mark Twain's major published works, except *Pudd'nhead Wilson*, a youthful and generally naive central character, whom the author calls an ''innocent,'' sets out on a course of adventures which teach him the ways of the world. The outcome of this ''initiation'' is a new awareness on the part of the innocent that the world is full of pain, repression, disillusionment, and viciousness, and that the free and naturally benign world of his youth was an illusion born of inexperience. In two of the earlier works, *Roughing It* (1872) and ''Captain Stormfield's Visit to Heaven'' (begun 1873), the hero moves away from a confined existence into a land of freedom and joy, but even these two reversals of the pattern employ the same characters, settings, action, language, and system of values found in the rest of the works.

The character of the innocent is compassionate, benevolent, and instinctively good. He has a natural desire to be free from all forms of external restraint. Although languorous and often downright lazy, he can be practical and quick-witted when occasion demands. He is often optimistic, unselfconsciously confident in the rightness of his internal promptings, and consequently sure of universal good will.

This innocent hero seems clearly to represent the American self-image which Evangelical Calvinism, the republican ideal, the pioneer

1

experience, and certain elements of romantic thought fostered in the early nineteenth century. He is the independent yeoman who derives his nobility from nature, the Evangelical Calvinist who recognizes his own emotions as the surest sign of divine grace, the American democrat who resists the artificiality and restrictive measures of social organization, and the pioneer *naïf* who trusts implicitly in the efficacy of his undisciplined will. He is the character we find Melville portraying variously as Ishmael and Ahab. He is Cooper's Natty Bumppo and James' Christopher Newman and Lambert Strether.

The setting in which Clemens' innocent heroes move is similarly symbolic, referring as it does to popular eighteenth and nineteenth-century attitudes toward the American landscape. At some point in his career, the innocent inhabits a "Delectable Land," an arcadian wilderness marked by freedom, purity, and spaciousness. Clemens often describes this primitive paradise as a wide prairie which resembles the sea, or a small village lying on a winding river near a virgin forest. Sometimes it is a broad ocean, sometimes heaven. It is almost always hazy, summery, and sleepy; and Clemens usually treats it as a dream. Occasionally it exists in the happy past, and it nearly always abounds in magic and mystery.

In contrast to this pastoral setting, we find in Clemens' stories of innocence scenes of urban, industrial civilization, with its schools, churches, armies, social classes, and businesses. The people who inhabit these civilized locales lack individuality and generally represent dominant social attitudes. They are lawyers, judges, priests, senators, soldiers, or common people banded together into a mob. They function as groups or as spokesmen for a group, not as free individuals, and they are deeply suspicious of social heretics who fail to conform to civilized opinions and values.

These two settings reflect that portion of the myth of American innocence which explained the self-determined good will of the American as deriving from the natural freedom of the new Eden, and attributed human failings to external pressures exerted by traditional institutions, rather than to innate depravity. The contrast between the goodness of nature and the evil of society recalls the ideas of men like Grotius, Locke, and Rousseau, who worked out of the very same line of thought which culminated in the myth of

2

innocence and taught Americans to see themselves as sinless, and external forces which sought to suppress their natural drives as evil. They are the ideas which guided Jefferson's domestic policies, which drove the pioneer to seek new areas of self-fulfillment in the Western wilderness, and which excited Middle-Western scorn for our wickedly-European Eastern cities as late as the nineteen-twenties.

In all of Clemens' works which recount the adventures of innocence, the hero moves between these two settings, and the movement constitutes his education, which we may define as the basic action of these stories. In most cases, the innocent begins his career in the happy land, free and blissfully ignorant. Circumstances then conspire to drive him into civilization, where he learns that innocence was a dream and that paradise is lost forever. Disillusioned and embittered with life, he longs for his vanished happiness and rails against the evils of his new estate. In *Roughing It* and "Captain Stormfield," again, the hero moves in the other direction, from repression to freedom, from civilization to nature. But in these two cases, as I suggested earlier, the values implicit in the settings remain the same. The difference is that the outcome is attended by a mood of optimism and relief, rather than bitterness and frustration.

While the character of the innocent and the Elysian and infernal settings reflect certain popular ideas about the American character and experience, then, the action—whether it be an initiation or a *de*nitiation [1]—is Clemens' own metaphorical comment on these ideas. The static picture of the innocent in the garden is rather commonplace stuff; it is the progress of the hero—from innocence to experience or from constraint to freedom—that constitutes the author's major contribution to the myth. The regularity with which the hero either trades his natural virtues for civilized vices or else goes down to defeat at the hands of society is thrown into sharp relief by the occasions on which he sheds his civilized identity and returns to his natural state of innocence. In the former instances, Clemens describes innocence as a desirable estate, but one doomed to extinction. In the latter, he shows the escape to be glorious and rewarding, but the escape is generally so fanciful that the accounts come off largely as extended pieces of wishful thinking. Clearly, Clemens considered the virtue of innocence highly attractive—an ideal which once held

3

great promise—but painfully out of place in the radically changing America of the nineteenth century.

Clemens underscores the values implied in the action by adjusting his narrative technique to the aims of each story, thereby apprising the reader of the attitudes he is to maintain about various characters and situations. He uses two types of narrative personae to relate the innocent's adventures—a reliable and an unreliable speaker. Because innocence in Clemens' work often suggests blissful, backwoods ignorance, and because his innocent hero derives in part from the vernacular figures of Southwestern humor, that character speaks in the vernacular whenever it is appropriate to his role in the story. Whether he uses this dialect or not, however, he generally reports only appearances; he does not often perceive the reality which is apparent to the author and the reader. For this reason I refer to this persona as unreliable. The informed adult who speaks for the author and reports the reality which lies beneath appearances, I call the reliable narrator.

Clemens combines these two speakers in different ways to fashion three related narrative methods. The reliable speaker may be an omniscient, undramatized narrator who reports both the reality and the naive views of the innocent—as in *The Gilded Age* and *Tom Sawyer*. Or, the reliable speaker may tell the story of his own boyhood, as in *Roughing It* and *Joan of Arc*. In this case, the narrator reports reality and appearances by shifting back and forth between the two personae as the occasion demands. Or, the unreliable speaker may tell his own story, foregoing the services of an explicit spokesman for the author, as in *Huckleberry Finn*. This method requires that the innocent report appearances and ''unconsciously'' suggest the reality beneath.

However Clemens employs these two personae in any work, their juxtaposed views create an irony which underscores the difference between the naive and aware mentalities, between innocence and experience. Furthermore, this difference embodies the essential meaning of the action—what happens to innocence as it faces experience.

Clemens developed the essential characteristics of this innocent

4

hero while serving a long apprenticeship in native humor, journalism, literary burlesque, and travel-narrative. His early works show evidences of the naïveté, the trusting nature, and the vernacular speech which identify the innocent in the later, major works. These early writings, beginning with his experiments with the traditional frame-story and ending with *The Innocents Abroad* (1869), also demonstrate a growing distinction between the innocent and experienced characters, and the evolution of the action and structure which are typical of the novels to come.

The line of development begins in the traditions of Southwestern humor, particularly in the frame-story.[2] In that narrative form an urbane, learned, aristocratic gentleman introduces a rustic, ignorant backwoodsman, whose vernacular speech and boorishness are calculated to excite the sophisticated reader's scorn. That is, the remarks of the educated narrator provide a "frame" for a self-portrait of the ignoramus. The cultured narrator is witty and fully understands the meaning of what he says; he is reliable. The bumpkin is funny, but he does not know it; he is unreliable. The aware speaker describes reality; the naive clown comments on the appearances that he sees. The reader recognizes the humor of the tale by perceiving the incongruity between appearance and reality, which is emphasized by the difference between the elevated rhetoric and the coarse dialect of the respective speakers.

The distinction between these two characters is, in many ways, similar to that between the experienced and innocent figures in Clemens' fiction. As we shall see, the reliable speaker of the frame-story emerges as either a dramatized or undramatized narrator in all of Clemens' major works, with the very significant exception of "The Jumping Frog" (1865), "Captain Stormfield" (begun 1873), and *Huckleberry Finn* (1884). His primary trait in those books in which he appears is, as in the frame-story, his ability to perceive reality. The vernacular character becomes, of course, the inexperienced young innocent. He also retains his most important characteristic—his unreliability, his habit of reporting appearance instead of reality.

Although these two characters appear together in "The Dandy

5

Frightening the Squatter" and separately in the letters of Quintus Curtius Snodgrass and Thomas Jefferson Snodgrass, respectively, "The Jumping Frog" is Clemens' first work of enduring literary merit to explore their comic possibilities. This is a frame-story insofar as it employs an articulate narrator who introduces a vernacular central figure, but there is an essential difference between this tale and its prototype. The urbane speaker in "The Jumping Frog" is no longer reliable; he does not perceive the humor of the matter he reports. Kenneth Lynn asserts that the vernacular speaker is playing a joke on the city slicker, and that this story constitutes an inversion of the values implicit in the conventional frame-story.[3] Mr. Lynn's analysis suggests that the backwoodsman has become aware of his role as a humorous raconteur and that he is consciously fooling the articulate speaker. Simon Wheeler is not so aware, however, for when he says of Smiley's mare, "The boys called her a fifteen-minute nag but that was only in fun, you know, because she was faster than that,"[4] he does not realize that in explaining one joke he has made another. Although Wheeler is not an object of derision (his speech makes him interesting rather than merely vulgar, and there is no longer a reliable narrator who can pass judgment on him), he is still incapable of perceiving reality. As a result, he is no more in control of the situation than is the urbane gentleman.

The important difference between "The Jumping Frog" and the old frame-story, then, is the disappearance of the reliable narrator. In the frame-story the author and the urbane gentleman were in complete agreement about the subject matter; they were, in fact, the same person. Clemens, however, does not appear in "The Jumping Frog"; neither the frame-narrator nor Wheeler speaks for him. Instead of explicitly describing reality, as frame-story authors did, he lets the two speakers unconsciously suggest the real situation which they cannot perceive. The reliable narrator of the old frame-tale has removed himself from the scene, and the unreliable character has been divided into a vernacular and a genteel speaker.

Three factors seem to have conspired to bring about this significant development. First, because of his vernacular speech and his craftiness, the rustic was inherently interesting; more so perhaps than the pompous dandy who dominated the stage in the frame-story.[5] As a result, writers had already begun to concentrate on the backwoodsman rather than on the gentleman before Clemens wrote "The Jumping Frog." Second, Clemens was skillful enough to establish the reality upon which the humor depends without having to state it directly through a reliable narrator. Third, he was already extremely interested in the naive voice when he wrote this story, for he had seen Artemus Ward act the "inspired idiot" on the lecture platform, and he had begun to deliver unpopular criticism in the *Enterprise* through the persona of the naive "Mark Twain."

The next time we encounter the burgeoning innocent, in Clemens' correspondence to the Sacramento *Union* and the San Francisco *Alta California* (1866 and 1867), a significant development has taken place. The reliable speaker is now dramatized in the character of a traveling reporter. The two unreliable speakers have assumed the traits of characters in literary travel-burlesque. The unreliable, urbane speaker of "The Jumping Frog" is replaced by a man who looks at the world through a haze of ideas learned from the sentimental romance, and the vernacular backwoodsman gives way to an unsentimental antagonist. The romanticist is called Mr. Twain, and his cynical companion is Mr. Brown. Together these two form a team in the tradition of Don Quixote and Sancho Panza.[6]

All three speakers—reliable reporter, unreliable romantic, and unreliable cynic—appear in this typical passage from the *Alta* correspondence. The narrator begins in the persona of Clemens the reporter, who gives a reliable description of the Nicaraguan countryside:

> About every two hundred yards we came across a little summer-house of a peanut stand at the roadside, with raven-haired, splendid-eyed Nicaraguan damsels standing in attitudes of careless grace behind them —damsels buff colored like an envelope—damsels who were always dressed the same way; in a single flowing gown of fancifully figured calico, "gathered" across the breast (they are singularly full in the bust, the young ones), and ruffled all round, near the bottom of the skirt. They have white teeth and pleasant, smiling, winning faces. They are virtuous according to their lights, but I guess their lights are a little dim.[7]

The speaker in this section fully understands the implications of his commentary. He is consciously witty, and the pun on ''lights'' is obviously intentional. There is no irony suggesting the speaker's inability to see the scene clearly. In addition, he controls his feelings on the subject. He registers mild approval by using such phrases as ''splendid-eyed,'' and ''pleasant, smiling, winning faces.'' But his similes (''like an envelope''), the prosaic details (''a little summer-house of a peanut stand''), and his pun prevent the tone from becoming overly emotional.

At this point the narrator dons the mask of the romantic Mr. Twain and continues the description. In keeping with his tendency to rhapsodize in the manner of literary romance, he says,

> Two of these picturesque native girls were exceedingly beautiful—such liquid languishing eyes! such pouting lips! such glossy luxuriant hair! such ravishing incendiary expression! such voluptuous forms, and such precious little drapery about them!

The crescendo rhythms created by the repeated exclamations indicate his excitement. The trite descriptive terms (''liquid, languishing eyes . . . pouting lips'') and the incongruous final item in the series suggest that the narrator is imitating someone so intoxicated by his feelings and his language that he is unconsciously making a fool of himself.

Mr. Brown then interrupts: ''But you prospect one of them heifers with a fine-tooth—,'' bringing ''Twain's'' reverie down with a thump. Brown's bad grammar and homely imagery accord with his role as the vernacular speaker. His harsh view of the scene shows him to be an enemy of sentiment. Furthermore, like Mr. Twain he is not aware that what he is saying is funny. He can see only ugliness, just as Mr. Twain sees only beauty. Both are unreliable, since both fail to see the whole picture. The irony becomes evident when their descriptions are compared to the reality that the narrator presents through the persona of the reliable reporter.

The three voices of the *Alta* and *Union* letters can be grouped in two ways, which help explain the transition from the narrative technique of the correspondence to that of *The Innocents Abroad.* First, Clemens (the reliable reporter) and Mr. Twain (the naive romantic) may be grouped together, since they are personae which the narrator assumes at different points. Brown (the cynic), then, is separated from these two by his dramatized identity and his vernacular language. Or, Clemens can be distinguished from Mr. Twain and Mr. Brown on the basis of reliability. Clemens is aware; Mr. Twain and Mr. Brown are not. In the correspondence the dialogue between Mr. Twain and Mr. Brown provides the important matter. But when Clemens revised the letters in preparing *The Innocents Abroad* for book publication, he dropped Mr. Brown and concentrated on Mr. Twain, shifting the emphasis from a conflict between sentiment and cynicism to the adventures of the inexperienced young traveler.

The naive character as he appears in *The Innocents Abroad* is a full-fledged innocent for the first time. In "The Jumping Frog" he was simply an unconsciously humorous character; in the *Alta* and *Union* letters he provided comic dialogue. But in *The Innocents Abroad* he is an optimistic, romantic youth who loses his illusions as he learns about reality. He inhabits for the first time an Innocent Land, and in this setting he begins to assume greater stature than he has previously exhibited.

He is not the central concern of this book, however. Clemens' initial aim in writing it was to set down "the record of a pleasure trip," and his method of composition resulted in a structure which prevents the innocent from rising above secondary importance. Clemens prepared *The Innocents Abroad* from letters which were written, sent off, and published in the newspaper while he was still making the journey through Europe and the Holy Land. Instead of using the letters as material for a continuous narrative, he maintained the epistolary form, so that each chapter in the book is still a resumé of a day's events, viewed from the end of that day. The narrative is a series of time-jumps; at the end of each leap the narrator recounts the events which have taken place since the last letter. Consequently, he does not describe his own initiation from a point outside the action, but exists within the time-span of the story and assumes either the voice of innocence or the voice of experience, as the occasion demands.

Although the epistolary form thus buries the innocent in the narrator and interrupts the progress of the initiation, the hero does display the rudimentary traits and perform some of the basic acts which become his trademarks in the later books. He adopts the innocent, unreliable persona, he betrays his optimism and his romantic bent when he begins his journey, he undergoes experiences which disillusion him, and he looks back upon his lost innocence after initiation.

The two voices are readily distinguishable in the first two chapters, which Clemens wrote at the end of the entire journey, instead of at some time during the trip. Because he has completed the trip himself, the initiate can describe the callow youth from a distance and contrast his own knowledge with the innocent's ignorance. For example, when the innocent learns the title of one of the passengers, he says,

> I fell under that titular avalanche a torn and blighted thing. I said
> that if that potentate *must* go over in our ship . . . it would
> be . . . safer to take him apart and cart him over in sections,
> in several ships.[8]

Then the narrator underscores the youth's naïveté by describing the same man from his adult point of view:

> Ah, if I had only known, then, that he was only a common mortal,
> and that his mission had nothing more overpowering about it than
> the collecting of seeds . . . I would have felt *so* much relieved.

The innocent reports how the passenger looks to him; the reliable narrator describes the potentate as he really is. Although the innocent's suggestion appears cynical to the reader, who maintains considerable aesthetic distance from the youth, it is ostensibly his sincere effort to solve a large problem. Consequently, the satire emanates from two sources: from the reader's awareness of how ludicrous the innocent's idea is, and from a comparison of the two descriptions. The passage not only satirizes pretension, it makes a careful distinction between the innocent and experienced viewpoints. Equally important, it shows that the innocent's attitude—erroneous as it may be —is superior to the inflated dignity of the mighty passenger and a source of more trenchant satire than the reliable narrator's more explicit comments.

Later in the book, when the chapters become periodic reports rather than chronological episodes viewed from a fixed point in time, the voices become more difficult to distinguish. In these chapters the narrator is being educated as the story progresses; he is not reporting an initiation that has already taken place. For example, he begins Chapter VIII with the hopeful ejaculation, ''This is royal! . . . Tangier is the spot we have been looking for all the time.'' He then describes his adventures in Tangier in the present tense, and closes the account with an expression of relief: ''I am glad to have seen Tangier—the second oldest town in the world. But I am also ready to bid it goodbye, I believe.'' [9] Obviously he is reporting the events as they occur. The sojourn in Tangier is an isolated unit and has only a sequential connection with the episode that follows. The narrator begins the tour of the town hopefully, reports its attractions and disappointments, and then implies his enlightenment by his desire to leave. The opening statement is innocent insofar as it is optimistic, and the closing comments belong to the initiate because they show disillusionment; but sustained irony, achieved by continually contrasting the naive and experienced viewpoints, is missing. Because the narrator still has plenty of disillusionments ahead, he is not aware enough at the close of this chapter to be called an initiate.

Imperfect as the narrative movement is, the innocent still undergoes an education which covers the entire span of the book. In the beginning he is optimistic. He is unsuspecting, since he fails to realize that certain advertised celebrities never intended to make the trip. He shows that he lacks prior experience when he breaks the most obvious rules of shipboard life. (Speaking as the reliable narrator, Clemens periodically confuses this characterization by interjecting autobiographical details—as when he mentions his own trip by stagecoach to Carson in 1861—but the fictive traits of innocence remain generally distinguishable from these bits of the author's personal history.) The innocent's credulity persists well into the book, for in the Holy Land he believes in the legend of the True Cross: ''When we listen to evidence like this, we cannot but believe. We would be ashamed to doubt, and properly, too. Even the very part of Jerusalem where all this occurred is there yet. So there is really no room for doubt.'' [10]

His adventures become a series of disillusionments about the romance of life. In Paris he learns that the *Grisette* is only a plain, uninteresting Frenchwoman, and says, ''Thus topples to earth another idol of my infancy.'' When he confronts the Bedouin in Syria, he recognizes that this terror and the travel-books' descriptions of him are frauds. When the book ends he is thoroughly disillusioned and remarks, "Travel and experiences mar the grandest pictures and rob us of the most cherished traditions of our boyhood." [11]

Clemens seems to get more and more interested in this innocent hero as the book goes on. Although the narrative emphasizes external details more than the growing consciousness of the innocent, and although Clemens is perfectly willing to use him simply as a narrative device and as a tool for satire, there is evidence that the author has begun to see the innocent as a figure with stature and symbolic power of his own. In the first place, Clemens grows increasingly nostalgic as the story goes on, telling several stories of a returned exile—Joseph, Jesus (whom he calls "a mysterious stranger"), the last survivor of the Seven Sleepers, and the Wandering Jew. These stories set forth the emotions felt either by the wanderer on his return or by the people of his home town as they compare his present state with his past youth. Then, Clemens comments explicitly on the glories of childhood. The Smyrna marketplace, for example, "casts [him] back to [his] forgotten boyhood," and makes him "dream over the wonder of the Arabian Nights." Finally, he describes the adult habit of selective forgetfulness: "Schoolboy days are no happier than the days of after life, but we look back upon them regretfully because we have forgotten our punishments at school, and how we grieved when our marbles were lost and our kites destroyed— because we have forgotten all the sorrows and privations of that canonized epoch and remember only its orchard robberies, its wooden sword pageants, and its fishing holidays." [12] These passages seem to me a clear indication that he was at least ready to see the innocent as the symbol of a desirable state of existence, and his comments about the disenchantment that experience brings suggest that he was beginning to think of the innocent as something more than an "inspired idiot."

The uncertain movement of the action and the amalgamation of the reliable and unreliable personae confuse the reader so, that he can never be sure who is responsible for which statements. Consequently, descriptive passages which typify the Innocent Land in the later books are scattered at random throughout *The Innocents*

Abroad. Still, they are instructive in that they exemplify techniques which become almost conventional for Clemens in his later descriptions of the Delectable Land.

In the first part of the book, the innocent escapes to the sea, just as the Greenhorn in *Roughing It* flees westward and Huck heads for the river. Away from land, he feels a sense of release and a natural propensity for benevolence: ''All my malicious instincts were dead within me; and as America faded out of sight, I think a spirit of charity rose up in their place that was as boundless . . . as the broad ocean that was heaving billows about us.'' [13] Expansive nature engenders expansive emotions in him. Large spirits are appropriate to this area of total possibility, the unbounded outdoors; and the further suggestion is that meanness is a product of confining civilization. This passage and his later comment, that the prairie is ''softer and smoother than any sea,'' show Clemens' tendency to operate in descriptive conventions also employed by Melville, Cooper, Parkman, and Whitman, who, as R. W. B. Lewis notes, often compared the prairie and the sea when discussing the freedom of the wide-open spaces.[14]

Clemens uses another detail typical of later versions of the Innocent Land when he gives Europe some of the dreamy quality that pervades Huck's river, Morgan's Camelot, and Eseldorf in *The Mysterious Stranger*. The narrator says, ''We have been in a half-waking dream all the time. I do not know how else to describe the feeling. A part of our being has remained still in the nineteenth century, while still another part of it has seemed in some unaccountable way walking among the phantoms of the tenth.'' [15] This passage also illustrates Clemens' early use of the dream as a bridge across time—the apparatus of *A Connecticut Yankee*—as well as the spectral details of Huck's and King Edward's worlds.

The narrator sees especially attractive scenery through haze and moonlight, which soften the harsh details and give the settings a fantastic atmosphere. Also, he describes legendary Palestine as a fertile, beautiful, dreamy garden. But he makes it clear that such beauties are all illusory, that moonlight is a fraud, and that ''war and commerce'' have turned this garden into a desert.

Although these descriptions are imperfectly integrated with the

13

innocent character, they suggest that in 1869 Clemens was growing interested in the innocent and his world. In the later portions of *The Innocents Abroad* he generally gives more care and attention to innocent illusion than to initiated awareness. The innocent's fancies are beautiful and exciting; the initiate's reality is ugly, tedious, and often vicious. Although Clemens recognizes that the moonlight on Gennesaret is a fraud, he still prefers it to sunlight, which reveals the brutal truth. The innocent is no longer merely a burlesque character, lampooning sentiment; he is the lucky inhabitant of a lovely, carefree land created by his own illusions.

To recapitulate this important development, the prototype of Clemens' innocent hero is the unconscious, vernacular character of the old frame-story. Clemens expanded this unreliable character to include both a vernacular and an urbane speaker in "The Jumping Frog" in 1865. He then gave these two figures certain traits shared by the companions of literary travel-burlesque, making the urbane partner a sentimentalist and the vernacular one an enemy of sentiment. In preparing *The Innocents Abroad* in 1869, he dropped the vernacular twin and concentrated on the naive, romantic traveler who doffs his illusions as he experiences reality. The reliable narrator in Clemens' work stems in part from the gentleman of the frame-story. This aware speaker does not appear in "The Jumping Frog," but rather stands aside with Clemens and the reader and laughs at both unconscious characters in the story. He reappears as a reporter in the *Alta* and *Union* letters in 1866 and 1867, where he and the romantic Mr. Twain share the narrator's duties. Finally, he is again a factual reporter in *The Innocents Abroad,* and once again he becomes one of the two personae assumed by the narrator.

Clemens developed an innocent hero, an Innocent Land, and a basic structural pattern as he moved from "The Jumping Frog" and earlier pieces to *The Innocents Abroad,* his first book-length work. The development of this character, setting, action, and narrative technique demonstrates his growing affection for the imaginative state of blissful ignorance, serenity, and ease; his increasing disgust with the disheartening realities of life; and his mounting interest in the fate which befalls innocence when it is made to face reality.

2.

The Greenhorn
and the Captain

ROUGHING IT and
*"CAPTAIN STORMFIELD'S
VISIT TO HEAVEN"*

ROUGHING IT and "Captain Stormfield's Visit to Heaven" mark three major advances in Clemens' treatment of innocence. They are the earliest works in which the hero is educated away from society into an Innocent Land. Second, Clemens fully dramatizes the innocent character for the first time in *Roughing It*. The hero is not only a narrative persona; he is a carefully defined figure. Third, Captain Stormfield is the first innocent to tell his own story in the vernacular.[1] Together, these two works represent Clemens' first purposeful uses of the character, action, and setting he employed so uncertainly in *The Innocents Abroad,* and they set forth attitudes and peculiarities of structure and style which reappear regularly as conventions in his later works on innocence.

In discussing *Roughing It* we must make a sharp distinction between the two volumes of the work, for although they deal with the same historical experience of the author, their themes and techniques are quite different. Volume One is largely subjective; it concentrates on the changes which take place in the hero as he experiences Western life firsthand. It is the story of the Greenhorn's flight from society to a land of mystery and great possibility. Volume Two is objective; in it the author directs his attention away from the hero, toward the setting in which he moves. The second half of the book is episodic and aims more at a literal representation of the West than at the development of the central character. In Volume One, setting and action contribute to the Greenhorn's awakening consciousness. In Volume Two, the hero calls attention to scenery and events by his comments, his moods, and his actions.

Theme, character, and structure are all implicit in the narrative method of Volume One. In a typical passage the narrator says,

> I was armed to the teeth with a pitiful little Smith & Wesson's seven-shooter, which carried a little ball like a homeopathic pill, and it took the whole seven to make a dose for an adult. But I thought it was grand. It appeared to me a dangerous weapon.[2]

Note, first, that the pronoun "I" refers to two people: the innocent, who is on the scene, and the aware narrator, who is recalling the events of the trip. The past tense, then, establishes the temporal distinction between the two: the innocent is clearly much younger. In the first sentence the narrator describes the pistol from the aware point of view, noting its absurd aspects. In the second, he sees the same pistol through the innocent's eyes, contrasting the Greenhorn's grandiose ideas with the reality already established. The two characters are distinguished by their respective points of view, and the aware speaker is relating his own growth from innocence to his present state of enlightenment.

The juxtaposition of these two points of view creates the irony which pervades the whole narrative, deriving its humor at the Greenhorn's expense. Since this tone asserts that the change from callowness to enlightenment is beneficial, the action is a tacit statement in favor of Western over Eastern standards. The narrator implies that the Greenhorn's delusions can only get him into trouble, that his inflated opinion of the weapon is foolish, and that maturity is infinitely more desirable. As the story unfolds, the Greenhorn sloughs off his old standards and his ignorance and takes up new standards and a greater perspicacity. The nature of these Western values explains why the innocent's progress is desirable in *Roughing It* when it was unfortunate in *The Innocents Abroad*.

The West in *Roughing It* represents freedom, release from constraint, and the disintegration of boundaries and limitations. When the Greenhorn leaves St. Joseph by stagecoach and enters upon the great Western Prairie, he leaves the "close, hot city" behind, gives up "toiling and slaving," and experiences "an exhilarating sense of emancipation from all sorts of cares and responsibilities." The narrator describes the plains in marine similes to emphasize their expansiveness: "Just here the land was rolling—a grand sweep of regular elevations and depressions as far as the eye could reach—like the stately heave and swell of the ocean's bosom after a storm." [3] Then he calls it a "limitless expanse of grassy land" and a "sea upon dry ground." Just as the ocean enables the traveler in *The Innocents Abroad* to exercise his benevolent instincts, the boundless Western "sea" helps the Greenhorn and an old friend forget their past grievances when they meet on the Continental Divide. That Clemens took this incident from an experience with his brother back in Hannibal rather than from recollections of his own trip west, suggests how much more interested he was in illustrating the ennobling power of spacious nature than in creating an historically accurate autobiography.

The characters the Greenhorn meets along the way display this same expansiveness and provide him with examples of conduct appropriate to this enlarged cosmos. "The Sphinx" shatters his civilized ideas about reticence among strangers. Although she is a burlesque figure, she is generous and friendly. The aristocracy of stage drivers, conductors, and depot agents signifies the value of personal accomplishment and character in a land which gives rank to capable men instead of to those fortunately born. The "first citizen" of South Pass City illustrates Western versatility and self-reliance by holding seven important positions in his town. Slade invalidates narrow conventional judgments, for he is both a desperado and a gentleman. Mr. Ballou furnishes a therapeutic dose of common sense when the silver-fever reaches its height, emphasizing the solidity and efficiency that comes from expanded knowledge; and Captain John Nye is the epitome of Western largeness and jovial confidence.

The West also provides experiences which strip the Greenhorn of his shallow optimism and romantic dreams, and his various awakenings are invariably described as fortunate. At the beginning he is "young and ignorant"; he has never been away from home. He is a "poor innocent" and expects to enjoy all sorts of exciting adventures in the West, foolishly hoping to be hanged or scalped. But as he moves through the West, he learns that the Indian is not a Noble Red Man but only a depraved and lowly Goshoot. Romance turns to reality as he crosses the desert, and naive optimism gives way to disenchantment when he learns that silver mining is largely drudgery. Each of these experiences weans him away from his romantic authorities and teaches him to see reality directly.

His education is desirable, then, because it makes him a part of this large, free, permissive land. Although he is an alien—an emigrant—when he begins his stay in the West, in time he becomes a member of a select society. As a Greenhorn he is inefficient and blind, but as an initiate he knows mining, milling, sharetrading, and other esoteric Western sciences. Shortly after arriving in Carson he is swindled into buying a worthless and dangerous horse, but after he has served his novitiate he participates in gulling a new Greenhorn in the Hyde-Morgan landslide case.

Besides being uncivilized and therefore free, the West has another quality which makes the hero's gradual awakening fortunate. Although his education is a steady movement away from illusion toward reality, that reality is not what it is in *The Innocents Abroad.* In that book illusion is false but desirable, since it softens the ugliness of evil reality. The "authorities" (the guide-books) deceive the traveler, but their lies are preferable to truth, which is tedious and hateful. In *Roughing It,* the authorities are romantic fiction, and although they too disguise reality, they are simply hindrances and have no redeeming qualities. The narrator of *Roughing It* never longs for his lost illusions, as the narrator of *The Innocents Abroad* does. In the European book, illusion is preferable to reality, in *Roughing It* just the opposite is true.

The reason for this difference seems to be that "reality" in *Roughing It* is not real at all, but almost entirely fanciful. The country is filled with apparently impossible phenomena. The alkali water at Scott's Bluff Pass is not really water; Soda Lake is "a *dry* lake"; and the Greenhorn finds a natural icehouse in the broiling sun. The land is unearthly, spectral, and mysterious. Before the stage driver is attacked, there is an ominous silence and then "the low wailing of the wind." The stage seems to stand still, although the passengers can still hear the grinding of the wheels. The attack itself is mysterious. Disembodied voices come from the distance, and when the incident is over it is never satisfactorily explained. The Pony Express rider comes and goes so quickly that he is like a "flash of unreal fancy," and the travelers never know if they have really seen him. When the jack rabbit runs away, he "mysteriously disappears." Snow in dead summer is "a mysterious marvel," and scenery is viewed "through the mystery of the summer haze." In Salt Lake City, awed by the Mormon settlement, the Greenhorn exclaims, "This was a fairyland to us . . . a land of enchantment, and goblins, and awful mystery." [4] Finally, the narrator emphasizes this air of unreality by describing singular events and scenes in the Western idiom of the tall story. Sagebrush, the coyote, and the jack rabbit are all depicted in the exaggerated style of the Western yarn.

These characteristics—spaciousness, freedom, mystery, fantasy, and idyllic beauty—combine to make the West of *Roughing It* the Innocent Land. As I mentioned earlier, the innocent moves into this land in all Clemens' books which deal with denitiation. In *Roughing It* the Greenhorn flees westward to escape the limitations and constraints of civilized society. In the West he is free to develop and to fulfill himself according to his natural abilities. As he loses his encumbering illusions, he becomes a part of this wonderful land and stands outside respectable society. The progress is clearly a form of escape from the unresolvable complexities of civilized life.

Volume Two, as I have already suggested, differs from Volume One in two essential ways. First, the hero is no longer the Greenhorn, but Sam Clemens of Virginia City, San Francisco, Tuolume, and the Sandwich Islands. Second, the author emphasizes, not the hero's personality, but the details of his environment. For these reasons, the second half of *Roughing It* has only oblique relevance to this study: it shows how Clemens' manner and attitude changed when he stopped developing a fictional character and began to write about factual events.

The central figure here is not the Greenhorn of Volume One. As we remember, that innocent had never been away from home and was totally inexperienced. The narrator of the second volume, on the contrary, explains that he has had a number of jobs, that he has been a printer, and that he has even been a river pilot between St. Louis and New Orleans. Except for the fictitious early jobs, the details are from Clemens' own life, as are most of the other facts in this second volume.

Just as the hero is different in the two parts, so is the author's main concern. In Volume One, Clemens concentrates on the developing consciousness of the Greenhorn; in Volume Two he directs his attention outward, toward the events and appearances of the West. This altered purpose is evident in the different emphases of the two volumes. In Volume One, Clemens builds up ironic passages by juxtaposing the naive and enlightened views, which represent, respectively, Eastern and Western standards. Because the action of the first volume takes place entirely in the West, the Greenhorn alone represents Eastern standards. Every statement he makes on the basis of his Eastern ignorance, therefore, draws attention to himself, since the civilized East is not presented for the reader's inspection except insofar as the Greenhorn embodies it.

But Volume Two emphasizes an entirely different matter. For example, when the narrator of part two discards his pistol, he says that he "had worn the thing in deference to popular sentiment, and in order that [he] might not, by its absence, be offensively conspicuous, and a subject of remark." [5] The statement is obviously ironical, because the speaker is not aware that going unarmed is perfectly acceptable practice in some parts of the world. Once again the irony depends on the clash of Eastern and Western standards, but this time the unconscious speaker moves in the environment for which he is spokesman. His statement results from his overexposure to Western violence, just as the Greenhorn's ignorant comments reflect his Eastern upbringing. But now the speaker draws attention more to his environment than to himself. He represents the West, its attitudes and commonplace situations, and Clemens uses him to emphasize the prevalence of mayhem in Virginia City. The gist of his remark is not that he is shy of public opinion, but that the public is quite accustomed to firearms.

The difference between the Westerner of Volume Two and the

Greenhorn of Volume One illustrates Clemens' uncertain attitude regarding the innocent. This Westerner is an innocent insofar as he is unconsciously amusing, but he functions exclusively as a narrative voice and a medium of ironic satire. He has neither identity nor capacity for development, and Clemens displays no interest in him beyond that which he always bestows on the naive voice of the "inspired idiot."

Despite the absence of a coherent narrative, however, the last half of the book shows repeated evidence of the author's attitudes about the comparative values of civilized and "natural" existence—inconsistent as these views appear at times. Pursuing his habit of following each description and anecdote with an evaluative statement, Clemens voices throughout this travel-narrative opinions which sometimes support the values implied elsewhere in his fiction, and sometimes reflect the conflict between progress and primitivism which troubled much of his adult life. As he relates his adventures in the gold fields of California, in San Francisco, and in Hawaii, he returns to the narrative techniques of the early newspaper correspondence, employing by turns the personae of the reliable narrator, the unreliable romantic, and the unreliable cynic.

The first thirteen chapters of Volume Two give an account of the "flush times" in gaudy and lawless Nevada, concentrating on the eccentric and ebullient personalities, the freedom and excitement of the place. Since Clemens has no central character to worry about here, the narrative becomes a series of anecdotes, tall stories, and descriptions in the local-color tradition. Like most of the works in this field, these chapters seem to have resulted from the writer's wish to capture a regional flavor that was passing as sectional boundaries disappeared. The familiar traits are all here: the dialect, the attempts to recreate atmosphere, the pervasive nostalgia, and the wealth of minute detail.

But these commonplaces of regional writing take on a special significance in Clemens' work; for while they are the stock materials of any local-colorist's craft, they become in Clemens' later fiction metaphors for the aspirations and disappointments he shared with large segments of his culture. The praise he lavishes on Captain Ned Wakeman, who jealously guards the right to administer justice against the intrusion of institutionalized law, bespeaks his faith in the individual's ability to do right without recourse to legal codes. His statement, "A crowded police-court docket is the surest of all signs that trade is brisk and money plenty," suggests his tendency to regard crime as a by-product of encroaching civilization. And when he argues that statehood for Nevada will kill the flush times by taxing the territorial residents into penury, he is lamenting governmental intrusion into private affairs and the resulting demise of freedom and carefree happiness. The bias illustrated in these passages pervades the tales of Virginia City in *Roughing It,* and it shows just how much Clemens was heir to the pioneer spirit—the impulse which drove men into the Western wilderness in search of freedom and opportunity for self-fulfillment and which kept them moving ahead of the civilization which inevitably pursued them.

Clemens leaves Virginia City to escape the restrictions on personal freedom which imminent statehood will bring with it. Entering California, he describes the Sacramento Valley in the same imagery which he used in the earlier works to convey a sense of repose and peace in nature, and which he would use again and again to paint the idyllic scenery of the Innocent Land in his fiction. Coming out of a pass in the Sierras, he looks down, "as the birds do, upon the deathless summer" of the valley, "with its fruitful fields, its feathery foliage, its silvery streams, all slumbering in the mellow haze of its enchanted atmosphere, and all infinitely softened and spiritualized by distance—a dreamy, exquisite glimpse of fairyland. . . ." [6]

In the valley itself, he comes upon ruins of the mining camps of 'forty-nine, which render him nostalgically eloquent on the romantic business of mutability. Oddly enough, the gold-seekers, whose Nevada counterparts were the free spirits of the territories, are despoilers of nature here. They have "torn and gutted" the pastoral landscape in their search for wealth, erected "gambling hells," and blasted the peaceful air with their "labor, laughter, music, dancing, swearing, fighting, shooting, stabbing. . . ." The metaphor has altered, but the referents remain the same: civilization spoils paradise with its avaricious, plundering, evil ways. Whatever the faults of the gold-hunters—and they paid for their greed by being "scattered to the ends of the earth . . . prematurely aged and decrepit"—they are better than the solid society which comes after. They "hated aristocrats. They had a particular and malignant animosity toward what they called a 'biled shirt.' " Although "disorderly" and "grotesque," their society was at least "wild" and "free." [7]

Clemens leaves the gold fields, practically overcome by nostalgia, and takes up residence in San Francisco, where he goes to work as a reporter. The humdrum routine of a regular job begins to wear on him, just as it did in Virginia City, so he seizes the chance to travel to Hawaii aboard the steamship *Ajax*. Like the true pioneer, he is susceptible to restlessness and suspicious of the demands which regularity makes on freedom. Although Western, San Francisco is just another oppressive city, and the chance to escape to primitive freedom is irresistible.

Arriving in Honolulu, Clemens lists a long series of descriptive details, setting the cramped and stifling atmosphere of San Francisco against the permissive languor of the Sandwich Islands. The passage begins with a reference to Diamond Head, with "its rugged front softened by the hazy distance," and ends with the summary: "In place of the hurry and bustle and noisy confusion of San Francisco, I moved in the midst of a summer calm as tranquil as dawn in the Garden of Eden." Gazing out to sea, he succumbs to "a slumberous calm and a solitude that were without sound or limit," and he finds it "ecstasy to dream and dream." [8]

Although he undercuts this revery with a cynical discussion of insect bites, in the old manner of Mr. Brown, there is little evidence that he was consciously building up a climax just to scoff at romantic attitudinizing. There seems to be far less distance here between the reliable narrator and the unreliable romantic than there was, say, in the *Alta* correspondence. In fact, there is no clear dividing line between the two voices. Instead of consciously shifting from the reliable to the unreliable voice in preparation for "Mr. Brown's" vulgarisms, Clemens seems to move naturally into the idiom of idyllic romance, only to become suddenly self-conscious and then puncture the inflated rhetoric which is apparently no longer under strict control. This tendency foreshadows Clemens' growing sympathy with the idyllic vision, the innocent's world-view. While perhaps false, it is at least more bearable than unswerving attention to painful truth. This development is one more step in Clemens' progression toward the naive point of view of *Huckleberry Finn,* which served him so well, and toward the incurable sentimentality of *Joan of Arc,* which resulted from his eventual inability to keep in check his tendency to romanticize the ugly facts.

His comments on Hawaii lead him into some curious inconsistencies, showing quite clearly the divided affections which caused him to vacillate all his life between nostalgia for his youth and hatred for sentimental sham. Speaking as the pioneer who, having been driven ever westward by creeping civilization, now stands in the middle of the oceanic frontier (toward which many of his contemporaries directed their Westering spirit when the continental frontier closed), Clemens laments the missionaries' success in civilizing the Polynesians. In a burst of anti-Christian anger, he remarks how happy the natives were "before the missionaries braved a thousand privations to come and make them permanently miserable by telling them how beautiful and blissful a place heaven is, and how nearly impossible it is to get there." These zealots, he goes on, ". . . showed [the Hawaiian] what rapture it is to work all day long for fifty cents to buy food for the next day with, as compared with fishing for a pastime and lolling in the shade through an eternal summer, and eating the bounty that nobody labored to provide but Nature. How sad it is to think of the multitudes who have gone to their graves in this beautiful island and never knew there was a hell."

On the next page, however, he earnestly extolls the virtues of the missionaries and concludes, unequivocally, that to gauge their success, one need only "compare the condition of the Sandwich-Islanders of Captain Cook's time, and their condition today." He then reverses his position once again, in a later chapter, and notes that the "purifying . . . contact with civilization" has "reduced the native population from *four hundred thousand* (Captain Cook's estimate) to *fifty-five thousand* in something over eighty years!"[9] It was no simple matter, in 1871 or in the future, for Clemens to decide absolutely between the benefits of progress, civilization, and wealth, and the happy state of natural innocence.

In spite of such lapses and inconsistencies, however, the themes of natural freedom and civilized restraint dominate the chapters on

Hawaii. The natives are innocents who "seem to have had a sort of groping idea of what came of women eating fruit in the garden of Eden. . . ." When the missionaries force them to wear clothes, they acquire vanity "as naturally as if they had always lived in a land of Bibles," showing thereby "evidence of a dawning civilization." Contemplating the natives, whose instincts have been perverted by artificial social codes, Clemens says, "Behold what religion and civilization have wrought." [10]

Clemens lives a life of "luxurious vagrancy" for six months in Hawaii before returning to San Francisco, and then to Virginia City, where the book ends. During the remainder of his stay in the Islands, he visits the more spectacular sights, most of which he describes in terms which suggest spaciousness, dreaminess, repose, and languor. When viewing the island of Hawaii from atop Mauna Loa, he says, one "could see all the climes of the world at a single glance," from "the bitter cold of winter" at the top to the "sultry atmosphere of eternal summer" below. Aboard ship, traveling between islands, he sleeps the sleep "vouchsafed to the weary and the innocent" as the moon beams "tranquilly on land and sea." When he looks from the rim of Kilauea into its crater, the fires "seem countless leagues removed. Here was room for the imagination to work! You could imagine those lights the width of a continent away. . . . It was the idea of eternity made tangible—and the longest end of it made visible to the naked eye!" [11]

Clemens seems to have identified this thrill of viewing vast areas of land through "mists" and "gauzy curtains" with the joy accompanying the release from both the biological limitations which restrict human perspective and the man-made obstacles which the city throws up to impede the vision. When the innocents of his fiction find themselves in the wide-open spaces which symbolize freedom and opportunity, they very often also find themselves a promontory affording wide vistas, hazy landscapes, and distant views of lands basking in perpetual summer. Distances open up for them, the paltry standards of scientific measurement cease to apply, and they feel themselves on top of the world. Occasionally, too, they experience a sensation of absolute solitude—a situation which points ultimately to the liberation of Theodor in *The Mysterious Stranger*. As Clemens expresses it, standing on the summit of the great volcano, ''I felt like the Last Man, neglected of the judgment, and left pinnacled in mid-heaven, a forgotten relic of a vanished world.'' [12]

Whether or not he concentrates on the developing consciousness of a central character, then, Clemens returns again and again to a set of steadily crystallizing attitudes about the ideal of absolute freedom and the reality of biological and social restraint. These attitudes, furthermore, tend increasingly to find expression in a set of images, settings, and phrases which seem to have come automatically to Clemens' mind as he considered his most pressing problems. The next opportunity to employ these conventions appeared to him as he set out to record the reactions of an old sea captain who visits heaven.

''Captain Stormfield's Visit to Heaven'' is an account of a denitiation narrated in the vernacular by the innocent himself. In the story, Captain Stormfield dies and goes to heaven, which he learns is a land of limitless possibility and freedom, and not the dull and restricted environment organized religion makes it out to be. ''Captain Stormfield'' is important to the matter of innocence because it is the first example of an innocent who relates his own adventures in the vernacular, and because in it Clemens explores again the desirable education of the innocent away from society.

The first-person narrative mode enables the reader to look at the action from a new perspective. In *Roughing It* the reliable narrator looks back on his own innocence and contrasts his present enlightenment with his past ignorance to create the irony. Because the vernacular voice is unreliable, however, Captain Stormfield can never be entirely aware. He cannot describe the reality which is the basis for the irony. So, even though he tells the story of his own denitiation after the fact, he always describes the action from the innocent's point of view. The reader, instead of standing outside the action with a reliable narrator—as in *Roughing It*—learns along with the deceived hero.

This technique makes it difficult for Clemens to establish reality, which he had done previously through an aware narrator. In ''Captain Stormfield'' the true situation, the reality into which the hero is introduced as he throws off his blinding prejudices, is described by accessory characters, whose only job is to explain to the hero what heaven is really like. The various gate-keepers, Sam Bartlett, and especially Sandy McWilliams, spend all their time disabusing Stormfield of his illusions about heaven. In this way Clemens can stick to the innocent's point of view and still communicate necessary information without having to work out complex ironies in the hero's speech. In fact, the rather mechanical use of reliable commentators is one of the story's main drawbacks; it makes unnecessary in Stormfield's vernacular the richness of implication that enlivens the speech of Si Wheeler and Huck Finn.

Aside from these difficulties, however, the narrative method of "Captain Stormfield" seems to have had two basic attractions for Clemens. In the first place, he could see the humorous possibilities inherent in an old sea dog's description of heaven. And second, the limited generalizing power of the vernacular enabled him to describe heaven in simple, concrete terms. Because the Captain is not concerned with the abstract properties of salvation, Clemens need not make complex metaphysical explanations. As long as all information comes to the reader via Stormfield's screening consciousness, matters beyond his very limited intelligence are necessarily absent. By looking at heaven through simple eyes, Clemens circumvented many difficulties which would occur to a more perceptive mind. Even Sandy, Sam Bartlett, and the heavenly officials can only explain as much as Stormfield can understand, since he reports their dialogue.

Stormfield has all the attributes of the typical innocent. Although he is probably around seventy, he is decidedly young in spirit; Clemens says of Ned Wakeman, the Captain's prototype, "There was no trace of age in his body . . . nor in his determined spirit, and the fires that burned in his eyes were the fires of youth." [13] As I have already noted, he is naive and speaks in the vernacular. He cannot see heaven clearly because he is burdened with the conventional attitudes of his society. Just as the hero of *The Innocents Abroad* had his guide-book, and the Greenhorn had his romantic novels and Eastern manners, Stormfield has the Sunday-schools' interpretation of heaven to deceive him. As he progresses through the story, he realizes the falsity of his "authorities" and learns to see heaven clearly and without illusion.[14]

The extract opens with Stormfield's death, which projects him into boundless space. Like the young travelers of *The Innocents Abroad* and *Roughing It,* he begins to behave according to the dictates of his naturally good heart as soon as he is free of his restricting environment. Flying through the air ''like a bird'' he meets Solomon Goldstein and immediately befriends him. He explains, ''I was trained to a prejudice against Jews—Christians always are, you know—but such of it as I had was in my head. There wasn't any in my heart.'' [15] The implication here is that man's heart is natural and good, and that his head is a repository of acquired social characteristics, which are bad. Away from society, man can obey his benevolent instincts rather than his reason.

Clemens contrasts earthly and heavenly values, to the former's cost, by having the obviously good-hearted hero believe that he is bound for hell. Like Huck, Stormfield appraises his own merits according to conventional civilized standards, which exalt the intellectualized and overweening piety of Talmage instead of the natural goodness of Solomon or Sam, his companions. The Captain learns later however that heaven values the spirit and not the letter of the Scriptures.

The environment which makes Stormfield's natural benevolence possible is Clemens' typical Innocent Land. The Captain's entry into it is mysterious and dreamy. The wind that blows over his deathbed sounds like ''a dream wind.'' He cannot rid himself of the idea that the whole adventure is a dream at first, and, of course, the whole tale turns out to be his account of a dream. Also, the boundless space of the universe is like the sea, a quality which calls to mind the ocean in *The Innocents Abroad* and the prairie in *Roughing It.* During his trip from earth to heaven Stormfield uses nautical terminology that is appropriate to both his mundane occupation and his new surroundings, and he even has a steamboat race with a comet. Later, when he and Sandy attend the reception of the bartender, they stand at heaven's gate and peer out over the ''ocean of space.''

Stormfield's education consists in casting off his erroneous opinions of heaven and finding what it is really like. He learns first that it is infinitely larger than he had thought, and that by comparison the planet Earth is a ''wart.'' Next, he discovers that harps, halos, palm branches, and eternal hosannahs are not so attractive in reality as they were in speculative Christian metaphors describing heaven. Also, after his initial shock at finding that heaven is not for earthlings alone, the realization that it is not limited to white Christians is less alarming to him.

His most important lesson is that heaven is exactly like earth, with one crucial difference: it imposes no circumstantial restrictions on individual fulfillment. All the states and countries of the globe are represented there, but, as if to symbolize the infinitely expanded possibilities which they offer, they are "a good many million times bigger . . . than down below." Natural geniuses who have been kept back by earthly circumstances finally take their rightful places of leadership and honor, and every man can behave according to his nature rather than as a slave to social determinants. Here Clemens reiterates the idea that natural goodness and genius are stifled by the artificial conventions and institutions of society.

The nature of Stormfield's heaven explains why his progress toward enlightenment is a happy one and why paradise can comfortably include industry, pain, and old age—states which Clemens usually found repugnant. Because heaven is limitless and imposes no restriction on its inhabitants, busyness is valuable and productive. Because happiness depends on sorrow, pain exists only for the sake of its opposite, and is not permanent. And because age brings usable wisdom rather than despair and death, permanent youth is not desirable. In short, because heaven, like the West in *Roughing It*, is essentially unreal, awareness brings fulfillment and not disenchantment. The "authorities" are as useless to Stormfield in heaven as they were to the Greenhorn in Nevada. Grateful acceptance sets the mood of this story, not rueful nostalgia as in *The Innocents Abroad.*

One more point needs to be made about "Captain Stormfield": Clemens' attitude toward the hero changes perceptibly as he sees him, alternately, as a buffoon and an enviable personality. Apparently, Clemens had two aims in writing the tale: to lampoon conventional ideas of heaven and to explore, in effect, the denitiation of an innocent. When Clemens concentrates on the former purpose, Stormfield tries out his wings and his harp, or Sandy McWilliams usurps the narrative spotlight with long explanations of the true heaven. But when Clemens invests his interests in his innocent hero, the

Captain exercises his natural benevolence or utters such engaging statements as, "My body gave out a soft and ghostly glow and I felt like a lightning bug. I couldn't make out the why of this, but I could read my watch by it, and that was more to the point." [16] As always, Clemens has difficulty maintaining a consistent attitude toward the versatile innocent, who can be so easily adapted to satire and who is so apt to degenerate into mere buffoonery.

In both *Roughing It* and "Captain Stormfield's Visit to Heaven," then, Clemens develops the theme of denitiation. Instead of looking back with longing to their lost innocence, the Greenhorn and the Captain happily throw off the encumbering prejudices of civilization and enter an Innocent Land full of mystery, wonder, and possibility. Both escape the limitations of institutionalized society and, by discarding its values and opinions, become capable of effective action in their new environment.

These two books also develop new narrative methods, which advance Clemens' art two more steps toward its culmination in *Huckleberry Finn*. In *Roughing It,* the author separates the aware and innocent sides of the central character by having the initiate relate the story of his own innocence. Clemens' new narrative technique enables him to isolate and develop his innocent hero—something that was impossible in *The Innocents Abroad*. In "Captain Stormfield," the author allows the vernacular innocent to tell his story for the first time, thereby releasing the humorous potentiality of the language and, at the same time, avoiding some complex intellectual problems.

3.

The Fallen Woman
and the Bad Boy

THE GILDED AGE
and *TOM SAWYER*

IN THE GILDED AGE and *Tom Sawyer* Clemens attempts to treat initiation as a fortunate circumstance, but because his sympathies are hopelessly divided, the experiment is unsuccessful in both books. In the former he was urged by his collaborator to turn an innocent into a tragic heroine by having her confront evil, but succeeded only in making her pathetic and sentimental. In the latter, the innocent joyously accepts wealth and adult responsibility, but he is, in the author's eyes, a failure as a man for this very reason. Clemens demonstrates in these two works his growing reluctance to see adulthood as anything but the absence of innocence, a time of senseless constraint and despair, and a state whose dominant emotion is nostalgia for lost youth.

These two books also mark two further stages in the innocent's rise from his early role as a satiric device, as in *The Innocents Abroad,* to his eventual position as a sympathetic central character, as in *Huckleberry Finn. The Gilded Age* is a satire on the irresponsible use of wealth by unscrupulous entrepreneurs and self-seeking legislators, but Laura's story is only faintly related to the major theme and even contradicts it in several respects. Her separation from the central theme strongly suggests Clemens' interest in the innocent as a character with a story of his own, distinct from any satirical applications. Similarly, Clemens originally conceived *Tom Sawyer* as a satire on boys' literature, but Tom's adventures are as much a boyhood idyll as a spoof on this subliterary genre, and Tom transcends his function as a character of parody. In the period of these two novels, then, the innocent is gradually freeing himself from the satiric function which contributed to his creation and is achieving an autonomy which will make satire secondary to the development of character in *Huckleberry Finn.*

Clemens' original aim in each of these works made him attempt two different reconciliations with the world which lies outside innocence. Laura acquires tragic potentiality by becoming acquainted with evil, and she decides to use her new knowledge to regulate her destiny and defy the world; Tom accepts his responsibility and approaches respectable adulthood. However, both of these attempts were futile, and Clemens only succeeded in strengthening his impression that life without innocence is either hopeless or, at best, reprehensible. Laura's amoral stand against fate ruins her, and Tom's willful acquiescence to respectability turns him into a hypocrite.

The Gilded Age, which Clemens wrote in collaboration with Charles Dudley Warner, is an account of greedy corruption in American government viewed, as Kenneth Lynn says, from the standpoint of educated, respectable Republicanism.[1] The final chapters of the book show that the object of the satire is the misuse of wealth by fools and unscrupulous opportunists. Although Ruth and Philip are made happy finally by money and love, Squire Hawkins, Wash, and Sellers are chastised for their foolish dreams of easy riches; and Dilworthy and the rest of the corrupt congressmen, for their avarice. And even though Clay and Wash ennoble themselves by deeds of self-sacrifice, they are ruined financially and consequently cannot be completely happy. Clearly, Clemens and Warner intended to satirize greed and the giddy hopes of affluence—not money, the object of those passions.

But Clemens' contribution to the novel, Laura's progress from innocence to despair and death, is an attack on money itself; and his expressed opinion that money is a symbol of lost innocence helps explain this contradictory line of development. Although he was himself constantly engaged in amassing a fortune, he habitually identified the Gold Rush of 1849 as the cause of America's downfall. In "Villagers of 1840-3," he says, "The California rush for gold in '49 introduced the change and begot the lust for money which is the rule of life today, and the hardness and cynicism which is the spirit today." [2] He looked upon his own youth in Hannibal before the Civil War as a time when no one cared for money, and said once of his boyhood:

> It was soft, sappy, melancholy, but money had no place in it. To get rich was no one's ambition—it was not in any young person's thoughts. The heroes of the young people—even the pirates—were moved by lofty impulses: they waded in blood, in distant fields of war and adventure and upon the pirate deck to rescue the helpless, not to make money; they spent their blood and made their self-sacrifices for "honor's" sake, not to capture a giant fortune; they married for love, not for money and position. It was an intensely sentimental age, but it took no sordid form. [3]

And in his autobiography he says, "In my youth there was nothing resembling the worship of money or of its possessor, in our region." [4]

His account of Laura's life reflects these attitudes, and he attributes her downfall to her forced introduction into an evil society whose only value is money. As she is dying, she does not long for a world in which people use wealth wisely but one in which money does not exist. Her adventures demonstrate that her death is not a punishment for her wickedness but the inevitable result of her initiation into a hostile, evil world over which she has no control.

When Laura first appears in the novel, she is a typical innocent, living in an idyllic, pastoral wilderness. Clemens establishes this setting as he describes the banks of the Mississippi River: "At night the boat forged through the deep solitudes of the river, hardly discovering a light to testify to a human presence—mile after mile and league after league vast bends were guarded by unbroken walls of forest that had never been disturbed by the voices or footfall of man or felt the edge of his sacrilegious axe." [5] Describing Laura herself, he says, "With all her pretty girlish airs and graces in full play, and that sweet ignorance of care and that atmosphere of innocence and purity about her that belong to her gracious state of life, indeed she was a vision to warm the coldest heart and bless and cheer the saddest."⁶ Notice that he employs traditional Christian vocabulary when he calls her girlish manners "graces" and attributes them to "her gracious state of life." Not only is she innocent, like Eve before the fall, but her innocence is natural to youth. Childhood, to Clemens, is a prelapsarian state and not subject to original sin. Man is born free from depravity and becomes evil through experience. Clemens repeats this idea later when he refers to Laura's fate as a fall from grace.

Notice, too, that her youthful purity gives her a "sweet ignorance of care." Clemens designates worry and responsibility as specific evils which accompany initiation. Furthermore, her innocence has regenerative powers; it warms and gladdens the heart. These three qualities—natural innocence, freedom from care, and revivifying warmth—reappear regularly in Clemens' innocents. Finally, like most of his innocent heroes, Laura is an orphan. When she enters the story her parents have been killed in a steamboat accident, and her past remains a mystery throughout the novel.

Clemens foreshadows this innocent's fall from carefree purity by giving explicit narrative asides and by describing initiation as the child's awakening from happy illusion to sordid reality. Immediately following the passage describing her innocence he says, "Could she have remained [innocent] this history would not need to be written." Her guardian's expectations of imminent wealth, unfortunately, are already preparing her downfall. Then, Clemens comments on the nature of childish disillusionment:

> In those days children grew up with the idea that stage coaches always
> tore and tooted; but they also grew up with the idea that pirates went
> into action in their Sunday clothes, carrying the black flag in one
> hand and pistolling people with the other, merely because they were
> so represented in the pictures—but these illusions vanished when later
> years brought their disenchanting wisdom. They learned then that the
> stage coach is but a poor, plodding, vulgar thing in the solitudes of
> the highway; and that the pirate is only a seedy, unfantastic "rough"
> when he is out of pictures.⁷

At this point, then, Laura's future history is outlined. She is innocent, but she cannot remain so because Squire Hawkins trains her to desire wealth.

Clemens now lays additional groundwork for Laura's fall by having her place her trust in romantic "authorities," representative of the naive illusions she forsakes when she finally awakens to a knowledge of evil. He explains, "She had more than her rightful share of practical good sense, but still she was human; and to be human is to have one's little modicum of romance tucked away in one's composition." [8] Her assiduous reading in popular sentimental fiction increases these natural romantic proclivities and gives her a false view of the world. As a result, when she learns that she may have a mysterious father roaming about somewhere, she begins to see herself as the heroine of her own romance. Still, she is an innocent, and her bookish illusions cannot dull her natural compassion; she forgets her selfish dreams when Mrs. Hawkins' distress excites her sympathy.

Prepared now by her vulnerable innocence, parental training, and romantic illusions, she begins to suffer the first shocks that the hostile world has in store for her. Evil begins to attack her from without, hardening her heart while destroying her fanciful visions of the world. When the townspeople learn that the Hawkinses are not her real parents, they begin to snub her. When her beau deserts her in fear of a scandal, Laura shows the first signs of the callousness that circumstances engender in her. "Poor crawling thing," she says, "I *do* begin to despise this world." [9] Instead of realizing that her romantic view is false and reconciling herself to the unfolding truth, she is merely disillusioned and seeks to remedy her early disappointments by immersing herself more deeply than ever in romantic fiction. But this reading only prepares her for the final shock, which Warner delivers in the chapters which follow.

Driven by the malice of her neighbors to seek escape, and led by her reading to expect a shining gentleman to rescue her, Laura falls in love with Colonel Selby, who seduces her and then leaves her. Had the chapters devoted to Laura's downfall been left to Clemens, rather than to Warner, the situation would probably not have dealt with a seduction. [10] When he wrote as a public figure, Clemens was ever chary of such matters, conventions of the sentimental novel notwithstanding. Still, there is no reason to believe that he did not approve of the situation as Warner advanced it. Warner's exposition was certainly genteel enough—the action all taking place well off-stage—and the seduction gave Clemens the chance to develop his views on the part sex plays in destroying innocence.

From first to last, Clemens' innocents are asexual—or more accurately, *pre*sexual. Usually the problem of sex does not arise, even when the setting would warrant it—as in the brothels of Virginia City and the saloons of the Mississippi riverboats. When it does, Clemens handles it cutely, as in the case of Tom Sawyer's puppy love; sentimentally, as in Huck's relationship with Mary Jane Wilks; or with open hostility, as in the sordidness of Huck's House of Death and the indecencies perpetrated upon Joan of Arc by her English captors. Except in *Pudd'nhead Wilson*, he does not seem to have been able to dissociate sex from dirt, especially when handling the sacred matter of innocence. *Pudd'nhead Wilson* frees itself from this limitation, apparently, by originating from sources outside the matter of innocence—sources which Clemens seems not to have fully explored or developed. Elsewhere, in *1601* and in his lecture to the Stomach Club, sex hides under that particularly unattractive guise known as "good fun" or, inaccurately, as "Rabelaisian humor." Even his comparatively free discussions of fornication in *Letters from the Earth* appear feckless and awkward, emerging as they do from a mind stifled by a lifetime of naïveté and beginning only too late to work itself free. What is more, he adduces his sexual evidence in *Letters from the Earth* to prove that God is unjust, and he maintains stoutly in the same work that Adam and Eve learned "sexual intercourse"—which he equates with "immodesty," "stain," "blame," and "offense"—by eating the apple.[11]

Clemens' obsession with the degrading nature of sex is similarly evident in *The Gilded Age*, where we see Warner contemplating for Laura a destiny altogether different from the one Clemens finally gives her. After her betrayal, Laura returns home and falls ill. When she recovers, Warner says, she is a new woman:

> And with her health came back her beauty, and an added fascination, a something that might be mistaken for sadness. Is there a beauty in the knowledge of evil, a beauty that shines out of the face of a person whose inward life is transformed by some terrible experience? Laura was not much changed. The lovely woman had a devil in her heart. That was all.[12]

36

While this passage remains largely a trite picture of the *femme fatale,* it indicates by its tone that Warner seriously considered the idea of a fortunate fall from blissful, pure innocence. Laura has experienced something of the retributive power of sin. Her initiation has given her added stature and interest by giving her a capacity for evil. Having confronted evil, she embraces it and decides to take command of her own life and use her new knowledge to fulfill the romantic dream of wealth and glory which had pervaded her youthful thoughts. She is willing to accept her new life courageously as personal tragedy, even when it no longer holds much hope for success. Unfortunately, as later events dictated by Clemens show, her belief that she can guide her destiny is also illusory, and malignant fate finally crushes her. Clemens apparently had no faith in her ability to use her knowledge in making significant decisions. Before the book is done, she learns that she cannot endure the malign forces of circumstance, and she pines at last for her lost innocence.

Laura's experience places her among Clemens' initiates. Unlike the Greenhorn and Captain Stormfield, who enter upon a fanciful world of possibility as they leave society behind, she learns the ways of the evil world with its constraints, cares and unhappiness. Her initiation is an awakening to "a knowledge of evil"; the devil has invaded her innocent heart. In her initiation she is like the Pilgrim of *The Innocents Abroad,* and like him she vanishes ultimately amid an atmosphere of melancholy. She is, finally, no more successful than he, for while Warner offered Clemens the opportunity to experiment with the possibility of a fortunate fall, he chose finally to consign her to inactive despair.

Laura's history from the moment of her awakening to the day of her death is a series of attempts to control the forces which conspire against her and to regulate her own destiny. But each experience only further convinces her that she is helpless. When she recovers from her illness, she yearns to leave home and become wealthy and famous in the city. Clemens says, "She detested the narrow limits in which her lot was cast, she hated poverty." [13] Eager to put into practice the feminine wiles she has learned from literary romance, she begins to look for a way to escape her restrictions. Harry Brierly suggests that she go to Washington, where she will be a great success and surely amass a considerable fortune. But she is unable to make the trip until the hypocritical Senator Dilworthy gives her money, as a loan against the fortune he expects from the sale of her father's land to the government.

The avenue of escape which she chooses, however, leads only to further confinement, disillusionment, and her eventual downfall. She is no less constrained in the great city than she was in Hawkeye. Her preformed opinions of the glamor of Washington and the stature of senators and generals pass away with experience. She soon begins to lose the last vestiges of her innocent youth—her rustic speech and her country timidity. When she takes up with Colonel Selby again, she learns the meaning of "the tyranny of marriage"; and when Philip asks her to break off those relations for the sake of Harry, who loves her, she says, "You can't make a life over—society wouldn't let you if you would." [14]

Having been driven to Washington by the pettiness of her neighbors, the hollow promise of her father's Tennessee land, the villainy of Selby, and the avarice of Dilworthy, she is forced by city society to assume the role of a heartless beauty; and in this role she kills Selby and goes to prison. Her attorney, Mr. Braham, tells her story to the jury at her trial, reviewing the external forces which have driven her to her present state. He says that she was "the loveliest flower in all the sunny south"; but "the destroyer came into this paradise" and "plucked the sweetest bud that grew there" and defiled it. He argues that when she came to Washington "relentless fate pursued her" as "the human fiend" tempted her again "to complete the ruin of her life." [15] Significantly, the main object of the defense is to prove that Laura, as the victim of circumstances, is not responsible for her actions.

Braham winds up his case by saying, "Society had pursued her, fate had pursued her, and in a moment of delirium she had turned and defied fate and society." [16] The plea wins Laura's acquittal, but just as her defiance of fate only increased her restrictions, her illusory freedom drives her to death. Once out of prison she learns that her father's land has not been sold and that her dreams of wealth are finished. Mrs. Hawkins begs her to return home, but she replies, "I cannot go back." Although she realizes that "fate has thwarted [her] at every step,'' she is still determined to take control of her future, to break with the past entirely and go on alone. She settles her hopes on a lecturing career, figuring to substitute ''the applause of the multitude'' for the love she has been denied. Fate refuses to yield, however, and after a churlish crowd drives her from the stage, she finally succumbs to her destiny and dies of a broken heart.

The action of the novel, then, traces the progress of Laura's character through several important stages of development. In the beginning, she is innocent, rustic, free, good-hearted, and happy. But external forces—all of which are urban social evils—rob her of her innocence and propel her into a life in which man rises by his knowledge of evil. In this second stage, then, she is awakened and, consequently, determined. Once she leaves innocent childhood, fate begins to guide her destiny and to pervert all her attempts to escape environmental restrictions. Laura is a tragic heroine at this point in her history, for she chooses to defy the forces which are driving her to destruction.

In the end, however, she is merely pathetic, as she finally gives in and chooses to die rather than to bear the responsibilities of her adult existence. Sitting alone in her apartment, she indulges in some sentimental maunderings about lost innocence. ''Her memory . . . lingered about her young girlhood with caressing regret,'' Clemens explains. That was the interval of her life ''that bore no curse.'' She sees herself ''in the budding grace of her twelve years, holding confidential converse with the flowers . . . when she was without sin . . . and unacquainted with grief.'' She closes with the same statement that Clemens himself made to Will Bowen's widow twenty-seven years later: ''If I could only go back, and be as I was then, for one hour . . . and then die!'' [17]

Clemens' final treatment of Laura is painfully sentimental and melodramatic, but it is extremely important insofar as it shows that he was not able to entertain a belief in a fortunate fall. Whatever stature Laura may gain from her defiance and cleverness diminishes as she indulges herself in these final lamentations. The knowledge of evil gives her strength at first, but her potentiality is never realized, and Clemens seems to deny the idea of an efficacious end to innocence. His sympathies lie, at last, entirely with rustic innocence and against civilized, urban evil. Even when one recalls the conditions under which the book was written (Clemens and Warner set out to show their wives that they could write a novel in the sentimental tradition that would be as good as anything the ladies repeatedly praised) and the fact that the two authors joked about its maudlin conclusion, the situations and language in Clemens' chapters are too close to those in such unrelievedly "serious" works as *Joan of Arc* for us to pass them off as a joke. When we recall how many American writers began by supposedly showing up the hackneyed manner of sentimental fiction for their wives' edification, excusing their own obvious interest in fiction by this ruse; and when we look back to passages in *The Innocents Abroad* and *Roughing It* in which an emotional outpouring is followed immediately by a deflating, self-conscious joke, we can see that the nervous laughter that tags after sentiment does not necessarily deny the truth of the sentiment. It suggests, rather, that the author had no language for sentiment that would leave him unashamed after it was set down in print. We have every right, I believe, to take the facts of Laura's story seriously, however unpalatable they may be, just as we must take seriously all the stupefying sentimentality of Clemens' later writing.

The Gilded Age, then, purports to be a conservative attack on the unethical manipulation of finance and its effect on our government. But Clemens' contribution to the novel shows Laura, an innocent, destroyed by the civilized institution of money. Through no fault of her own she becomes an exile, a *femme du monde,* and a murderess; and fate finally drives her to death from the effects of excessive despair. Although Clemens may have intended his heroine to illustrate the thesis of the book, in the end she demonstrates the impossibility of effective action in a world devoid of innocence. By developing Laura's character separately from the theme of the novel, Clemens shows his growing awareness of the innocent as a character with an interest of his own, aside from his ability to embody a satirical point of view. And by sending Laura to her death at the end of *The Gilded Age,* he foreshadows his future disinclination to deal with the problems of life without innocence.

Even with this unfortunate experiment behind him, Clemens

wrote *Tom Sawyer,* in which he once again attempted to portray a successful initiation. But in this work the hero's final disposition results from the clash of conflicting themes, not from Clemens' apparent disinclination to show innocence achieving new stature and dimension by confronting evil. The book contains three distinct themes, and these stem from three aims which led Clemens to write it. In the first place, *Tom Sawyer* is a revision of "A Boy's Manuscript," which is largely an adult's amused view of childhood. Second, Clemens set out to recreate his own boyhood as he remembered it, to portray innocence with all the attractions which Laura remembers in her death scene. Third, since Clemens wanted to show that a bad boy could succeed as well as the good boys of pietistic children's fiction, he told a story in which a boy attains wealth and respectability even though he has all the traits which the conventional works condemned.[18] The first of these aims contributes nothing to the second; and the last two work against each other, for Tom's eventual reconciliation with the forces of adult, civilized society— which the satire on the successful good-boy demands—violates Clemens' basic distrust of society, which prompted him to celebrate natural innocence in the first place.

This conflict causes Clemens repeatedly to shift his opinion of his hero. When Tom is a child in an adult's world, he is foolish and earns the reader's tolerant amusement. When he is an innocent, he is sympathetic, an object of admiration and envy. And when he is a candidate for respectability, a burgeoning citizen, a bad boy who is on his way to making good, Clemens treats him with contempt and even hostility.

These attitudes appear in the novel as three different points of view. When Tom is a foolish boy, a holdover from "A Boy's Manuscript," Clemens poses as an amused adult, who is close to the reader and detached from his hero. When Tom is an innocent, Clemens identifies himself with the boy, attends closely to his unspoken thoughts and emotions, and sees the world through Tom's eyes. And when Tom is in the process of succeeding, Clemens again stands detached from him; but in this case the author is not the amused adult but someone who agrees with Huck Finn in the final chapters.

Clemens' opinions of the book after its completion encourage a search for such internal conflicts. In a letter to Howells, he says that the book is finished and that he will not carry Tom beyond boyhood: "If I went on, now, and took him into manhood, he would be just like all the one-horse men in literature and the reader would conceive a hearty contempt for him." [19] * He says elsewhere that the boy would grow up to be "an ordinary liar," and in an interview with Kipling he remarked, "I had a notion of writing the sequel to *Tom Sawyer* in two ways. In one I would make him rise to great honor and go to Congress, and in the other I should hang him." [20] Another comment to Howells suggests that the difficulty lies in the narrative mode Clemens used in writing *Tom Sawyer*. He says in the letter quoted above, "I perhaps made a mistake in not writing it in the first person . . . By and by I shall take a boy of twelve and run him through life (in the first person) but not Tom Sawyer—he would not be a good character for it." [21] * Apparently Clemens was satisfied with that part of the novel which he related through Tom's eyes but not with those portions which he told as a detached observer. Significantly, the passages which stick most closely to Tom's point of view are those which portray him as an innocent—those which see him without treating him as a childish buffoon or as a reprehensible adult.

The conflicts which account for Tom's changing nature can be illuminated, I believe, by an examination of passages from the novel in which the three points of view are apparent. This analysis can also provide some useful information about Clemens' developing method of handling the matter of innocence; and it can help to explain why he selected Huck as the boy to tell his own story in the sequel to *Tom Sawyer*.

In those portions of the narrative in which the author is most sympathetic to Tom, the boy is a typical innocent. He is an orphan, and although Aunt Polly refers once to her "own dead sister," she never mentions his father or other details of his origin. Tom's main desire is to be free, and he looks at the institutions of St. Petersburg —school, church, family—as "captivity and fetters." His aunt punishes him with "captivity at hard labor," and his first act in the book is to attempt an escape. There is a restraint about "clothes and cleanliness that galled him,'' and on Jackson's Island he goes naked. Furthermore, the restraint of the town is not entirely of his own imagining, for Clemens says that the strain of memorizing scriptures drove the German boy insane and that a sermon ''dealt in limitless fire and brimstone and thinned the predestined elect down to a company so small as to be hardly worth the saving.''

As an innocent, Tom has a good heart. He tells Jim not to mind Aunt Polly's scolding: ''She talks awful, but talk don't hurt—anyways it don't if she don't cry.'' [22] When she weeps over him for his mischief, it is ''worse than a thousand whippings'' to him. His native compassion has the most room to operate during his escape into the wilderness of Jackson's Island. Returning home, he sees Aunt Polly asleep in her chair, and ''his heart [is] full of pity for her.'' Later he relieves her sorrow about his failure to let her know that he was not dead but only ''run off.''

Passages which typify Clemens' close personal handling of his hero are those in which Tom contemplates unspoiled nature. As an innocent, his proper domain is the uninhabited countryside; and although the entire setting of the novel provides escape by carrying the reader back to a sinless ''canonized epoch,'' Clemens distinguishes between the innocent woods and fields and the evil town within the larger context. He describes Jackson's Island through Tom's eyes, underscoring the innocent's kinship with nature. As the boy sits basking in ''a delicious sense of repose and peace,'' he watches a measuring worm crawl over him, talks to a ladybug, and touches a tumblebug. A catbird sings to him, and a jay and a squirrel come within his reach unafraid. Similarly, when the innocent is trapped in the town, he looks out of the school window, and Clemens describes both the summer scenery and Tom's longing to be free: ''Away off in the flaming sunshine Cardiff Hill lifted its soft green sides through a shimmering veil of heat, tinted with the purple of distance; a few birds floated on lazy wing high in the air; no other living thing was visible but some cows, and they were asleep.'' [23]

As long as Clemens treats Tom as an innocent, he maintains this idyllic, rustic setting. Like the Innocent Land of *Roughing It* and ''Captain Stormfield,'' and of Laura's memories in *The Gilded Age*, it is dreamy, fanciful, hazy. When the boys run off, Jackson's Island becomes the primeval wood which offers escape from civilized constraint. Their trip there is a momentary denitiation, since they turn their backs on society, casting off their clothes and behaving like savages. Clemens describes their exploring expedition: "They tramped gaily along, over decaying logs, through tangled underbrush, among solemn monarchs of the forest, hung from their crowns to the ground with a drooping regalia of grapevines. Now and then they came upon snug nooks carpeted with grass and jeweled with flowers." [24] This blissful garden is the appropriate setting for the innocent, as is Cardiff Hill, which the author describes as a "Delectable Land," far from the village, "dreamy, reposeful, inviting."

Tom Sawyer is full of magic and the supernatural. Superstition, as Walter Blair remarks, is an appropriate element in the boy's story because it was so prevalent in the author's own childhood.[25] Clemens' attention to ghostly atmosphere in all his books about innocence may result from his recollections of his own boyhood. Furthermore, magic in *Tom Sawyer* is confined almost exclusively to the boy's world, and it generally works best away from the village. Huck's remedy for warts requires that the afflicted go into the woods, and Tom's rituals for finding lost marbles and for communing with the doodlebugs are effective on Cardiff Hill. Magic and spectral portents surround the boys' most important adventures: the night in the graveyard, the search for the treasure, and the eventual discovery of gold in MacDougal's Cave.

As an innocent, then, Tom lives in an idyllic world of freedom and wonder; and as an innocent he has stature which transcends his importance as a mischievous backwoods boy. Clemens provides him with virtual symbolic status by attending seriously to his innocent qualities of isolation, good-heartedness, and freedom.

Probably the best example of Tom as a foolish youngster appears in the passage in which the lovesick boy moons over the "Adored Unknown" and lies down beneath her window. This episode is a revised portion of "A Boy's Manuscript"—as are most of the early encounters between Tom and Becky. Clemens' rather patronizing attitude toward Tom in these sections apparently stems from the earlier version. This attitude is evident not only in the boy's ridiculous antics, which separate him from the adult's world and invite the reader's good-natured amusement, but in the author's language as well. Although Clemens attunes his ear to Tom's innermost feelings in this passage he reports these emotions in a language that mocks the boy and encourages the reader to smile knowingly on the absurdly romantic youth. For example, he calls Tom a "poor little sufferer" and a "martyr"; he makes him use a string of hollow clichés to report his "dismal felicity." These sketches of Tom's childishness provide a good beginning for the hero who is to mature, but neither his youth nor his maturity is compatible with his innocence. The former precludes the sublimity of innocence, and the latter denies the basic qualities of that state.

That side of Tom's character which emerges from Clemens' desire to depict the successful bad boy is distinctly not innocent. In the whitewashing episode Tom behaves like an unscrupulous entrepreneur, taking advantage of his fellows for personal gain. After duping Ben Harper, he sits on his barrel, munching his apple and planning "the slaughter of more innocents." In the course of the day he "bankrupts" every boy in the village, and so rises from the position of a "poverty-stricken boy" to that of a capitalist "literally rolling in wealth." His business venture at Sunday school is similarly profitable. At the beginning he tries to learn his lessons "under the double pressure of curiosity and prospective gain." Mary satisfies both when she gives him a knife for his trouble. At church he trades "the wealth he had amassed in selling whitewashing privileges" for tickets on the prize Bible. When he claims the reward, his victims appropriately call him "a wily fraud, a guileful snake in the grass." His speculation appears especially unattractive when we learn that Mary, an unswervingly sympathetic character, acquired two Bibles by "the patient work of two years."

Tom progresses in the book from carelessness to responsibility. Walter Blair says, "Each of several lines of action begins with Tom's behaving in an irresponsible childish fashion and ends with an incident signifying his approach to responsible maturity." The trouble is that with approaching maturity Tom becomes a respectable and accepted figure in St. Petersburg society. Walter Blair illustrates Tom's progress by saying, "At the end, in a conversation with Huck, Tom, although still a boy, is talking very much like an adult." [26] In that dialogue Tom is trying to convince Huck to become respectable, too. Huck complains about the constraint and regularity of the Widow's routine and says that he can't stand it. Tom explains, ''Well, everybody does that way, Huck''; and Huck counters, ''Tom, it don't make no difference. I ain't everybody.'' [27] Clemens' sympathies are clearly with Huck in this exchange, for the unregenerate boy is asserting his right to be a free individual while Tom has gone over to the other side; he has sold out his freedom and innocence for acceptance and security. Earlier in the book Tom was the bad boy, but by the end the townspeople treat him as one of themselves. Judge Thatcher has plans for Tom to be ''a lawyer or a great soldier'' and to send him to the ''National Military Academy.'' He has the boy's money out at six percent, giving him a comfortable income.

But while Tom has capitulated, Huck remains true to his innocent desire to be free. He is appalled at Tom's plans to get married, and swears that he will never let a girl ''comb'' him. Again Clemens is on Huck's side in the argument. These conversations in which Tom argues for convention and Huck remains skeptical foreshadow the respective characters the two boys will take in *Huckleberry Finn.*

There is evidence throughout the novel of the author's increasing interest in Huck; he must have had this boy in mind when he told Howells that he wanted to tell a boy's story in the first person. Huck's main attraction for Clemens, it seems, is his refusal to be initiated, for although he accepts his half of the money and agrees to return to the Widow's (presumably for the sake of a tidy ending), he begins his own story by giving up the money and leaving the Widow again. He has been the symbol of freedom since the first of *Tom Sawyer.* He has ''everything that goes to make life precious,'' in the opinion of ''every harassed, hampered, respectable boy in St. Petersburg.'' He is democratic, for he eats with the Negroes, although civilized convention frowns on such fraternizing.

Clemens seems to have recognized by this time, at least vaguely, that in order to keep his innocent from being sullied by the comments of the adult narrator, he would have to let him tell his own story. At the end of the novel, the author is obviously disappointed with Tom, whom he has forced into conformity and respectability; but Huck already has many of the attractions which would make Clemens select him as the hero of the sequel. *Tom Sawyer* is the story of an initiation into society; *Huckleberry Finn* would take up the escape theme again. However appealing the former book may be to the reader, it was unsatisfactory to Clemens, for it pointed toward the same fate that Laura had suffered, and it ends with Tom's blind acceptance of the adult responsibility which the author had tried to throw off by writing it.

Tom Sawyer, with its nostalgic setting, then, seems to be Clemens' objectification of Laura's lost world of innocence. But the serpent creeps into St. Petersburg just as it did into Hawkeye, and once again it comes in the form of money. Because he wanted to make Tom a bad boy who emerges accepted and respectable from his irresponsible childhood, he destroyed his hero's innocence. Clemens' experiments in *The Gilded Age* and *Tom Sawyer,* unsuccessful as they are in certain respects, were not altogether fruitless, however, for out of the two books he salvaged a hero, a point of view, and a setting, which would provide a basis for *Huckleberry Finn.*

4.

The Cub,
the Changeling
and the Recruit

"OLD TIMES ON THE MISSISSIPPI,"
THE PRINCE AND THE PAUPER
and *"A CAMPAIGN THAT FAILED"*

THERE ARE several reasons for discussing "Old Times on the Mississippi," *The Prince and the Pauper,* and "The Private History of a Campaign that Failed" in the same chapter. Clemens wrote the first two of these before he completed *Huckleberry Finn*—the second while that novel was in progress—and he wrote the third shortly after its publication; so they all shed some light on the great book.[1] Second, all three works recount the adventures of an innocent who flees from an environment of constraint into the land of his dreams and then awakens to find his dreamland filled with disappointments. The hero's progress is, then, ultimately initiatory, a progress toward the ugly truth, as it is in *The Gilded Age,* not denitiatory, as in *Roughing It.* Third, the three works demonstrate Clemens' habit of cutting off the story of an initiation at the moment of the innocent's awakening—a tendency which indicates a good deal about his attitude toward innocence.

In "Old Times"[2] the initiate tells the story of his own innocent years from a point of view outside the action, just as the Old-timer does in *Roughing It*. The narrator adopts the reliable-adult and unreliable-innocent personae as the occasion demands. In this way he can juxtapose the reality and the appearance to give two views of the action—one objective and one involved, one from outside the action and one within. For example, when he describes a "cheap, gaudy packet . . . from St. Louis," he is looking at the river from a reliable, detached point of view. But when, in the same passage, he calls the paddleboxes "gorgeous," the captain "imposing," and the boat "handsome," [3] he is seeing these things through the boy's eyes. By assuming these two identities in a single description, the narrator not only dramatizes the external events, but defines the innocent character by contrasting the youth's happy illusion with what Clemens believes to be the truth.

In the first section of "Old Times," the innocent envies his companions who have escaped from the humdrum village and become part of the glamorous life on the river. The river symbolizes for him the chance to rise above the circumstances in which fate has cast him; to go on the river is to escape provincial mediocrity. That his parents refuse to let him become a steamboatman and cause him to run away, is significant, for although "Old Times" purports to be Clemens' account of his own life on the river, he did not run away from home to become a pilot. Clemens seems to have intended to emphasize the need for escape by including this detail, just as he freely manipulated autobiographical fact in *Roughing It* in order to attain desired effects.

In the second section, the young hero betrays the several traits which establish his innocence. He is ignorant and optimistic, for he plans to explore the Amazon on thirty dollars. As a deck passenger he is the lowliest creature on the river. Whatever he may have been on land, like the emigrant in the West and the newcomer in heaven, he is demeaned by his ignorance of his new surroundings. He is so low, in fact, that he considers it an honor to listen to the watchman's sentimental ramblings. Like the Pilgrim of *The Innocents Abroad* and the Greenhorn of *Roughing It*, he has romantic ideas about travel; he has not yet learned what the Pilgrim discovers, that "travel and experience . . . rob us of the most cherished traditions of our boyhood.'' Then, a native of the new world into which he is being initiated dupes him: a passenger persuades the innocent to lend him some money and never returns it. This incident corresponds to the one in *The Innocents Abroad* in which the European girl sells the Pilgrim a worthless pair of gloves, and the one in *Roughing It* in which the Carson sharper sells the Greenhorn the Mexican plug.

The innocent finally persuades a pilot to take him on as a cub and so begins his formal education. Piloting has a twofold attraction for him: it is filled with glory and romance, which will make him the envy of his village when he returns, and it is the freest profession on earth. The innocent seeks freedom by pursuing his romantic dreams of glory. His initiation makes him realize that freedom is illusory; it vanishes with his dreams.

As he learns the ways of the river, he is most dismayed by the prodigious and unending job that faces the pilot in keeping up with the changing shape of the stream. He cannot simply learn the river and let it go at that; he must know it both upstream and downstream, by day and by night, and he must keep abreast of its rapidly changing course. One of his main lessons is that the pilot earns his ''freedom'' by dedicating himself to his endless task.

The movement of the action, consequently, is complex. On the one hand, the innocent progresses toward a kind of desirable awareness, for by learning the river he becomes a part of a society that is free from social restraint. Like the Greenhorn and Captain Stormfield, the Cub becomes effective as he learns the ways of his new environment. However, by learning to ''read'' the river, the Cub also discovers that details which he once thought beautiful are actually signs of danger.

> Now when I had mastered the language of this water and had come
> to know every trifling feature that bordered the great river as
> familiarly as I knew the letters of the alphabet, I had made a valuable
> acquisition. But I had lost something, too. I had lost something which
> could never be restored to me while I lived. . . . No, the romance and
> beauty were all gone from the river. All the value any feature of it
> had for me now was the amount of usefulness it could furnish
> toward compassing the safe piloting of a steamboat. Since those days,
> I have pitied doctors from my heart. What does a lovely flush in a
> beauty's cheek mean to a doctor but a "break" that ripples above some
> deadly disease? Are not all her visible charms sown thick with

what are to him the signs and symbols of hidden decay? . . . And doesn't he sometimes wonder whether he has gained most or lost most by learning his trade? [4]

The pastoral vision of nature vanishes; the realistic vision, which sees nature as a malign force threatening to sink the steamboat, takes its place. While the innocent has been progressing hopefully toward freedom, he has actually been courting disaster.

The initiation in "Old Times" is comparable to that in *The Innocents Abroad:* both are awakenings to a knowledge of natural evil. To the innocent the cosmos is benign, idyllic, full of possibility, romantic, and joyful. But to the initiate it is malevolent, constraining, harshly realistic, and sad. The Cub's sense of loss is unmistakable, and it creates a nostalgic mood that was also present in *The Innocents Abroad,* but not in *Roughing It* or "Captain Stormfield." "Old Times" does not move away from reality, as do the two works on denitiation, but toward it. Instead of exploring the possibility of freedom and fullfillment through awareness, it describes the disenchantment that follows the loss of illusion.

The "authorities" in *Roughing It* and "Captain Stormfield" were useless and happily discarded. In "Old Times" the romantic, aesthetic view of the river and childhood dreams of glory—the "authorities"—are, like the illusions of *The Innocents Abroad,* in many ways preferable to the truth. Also, while the Captain and the Greenhorn leave civilization and enter the infinitely expanded, dreamy, mysterious Innocent Land, the Cub passes out of the Innocent Land when he loses his vision of its idyllic beauty and begins to perceive real evil. Both "Old Times" and *The Innocents Abroad* make a false start toward freedom and fulfillment: the Pilgrim enjoys a feeling of release when he goes to sea, and the Cub seems to be progressing toward the free state of pilothood. But the real world in which each moves will not support the illusion of space and benignity that is needed to perpetuate natural innocence. Consequently, the two heroes pass out of innocence and end in despair and disenchantment.

Like all of Clemens' early accounts of innocence, "Old Times" subordinates character to setting. The Pilgrim, the Greenhorn, the Captain, and the Cub owe their existence to Clemens' desire to discuss Europe, the West, heaven, and the Mississippi, respectively.

But in each of these works the hero receives a little more attention than in the one previous, and—except for Captain Stormfield, who is the result of many revisions after 1875—the Cub in "Old Times" is more fully developed than any innocent who precedes him. As Clemens continued to use the awakening innocent to organize "local color" material, he gave more and more care to the innocent's character and point of view.

The twin heroes of *The Prince and the Pauper* continue in this line of development and profit from the important step toward centrality taken by Tom Sawyer. Although Clemens originally conceived *Tom Sawyer* partly as a literary satire and partly as an imaginative sojourn into youth, the hero is more than just a bad boy who makes good, and he is just as important as the idyllic setting in which he moves. That is, the book is as much about Tom Sawyer as a person as it is about children's literature or prewar Hannibal. But while Tom had to fight his way through Clemens' original aims to thematic supremacy, Tom Canty and Edward seem to have started there.

The Prince and the Pauper, then, is a story of two innocents first, and only secondarily a satire on monarchy. Because of this emphasis Clemens never treats Tom and Edward as buffoons. The book is the account of Tom's and Edward's twin fates. Both escape from their restricting native environments into a land which was free and happy in their dreams but which turns out to be confining and evil in reality. Ironically, the dreamland which each longs for is the situation which the other wants to escape. The final meaning of the action is that freedom and perpetual innocence exist only in dreams; when these are shattered, disenchantment follows. The situation is not entirely hopeless, however, as the narrative technique, characterization, and action indicate.

The narrator of *The Prince and the Pauper*—like those in *Tom Sawyer* and *The Gilded Age*, and unlike those in *The Innocents Abroad*, *Roughing It*, "Captain Stormfield," and "Old Times"—is undramatized. He is to this extent a conventional third-person narrator, but his attitudes and his point of view relate him directly to the theme of the novel. He is actually an initiate, although he himself is never an innocent, as the narrator of *Roughing It* was. He is cynical and misanthropic; for example, he describes the parliament as "slavish" and the London rabble as "human vermin." Being reliable, he sees reality clearly, and the reality he sees is evil. Since the innocent's fate, always, is to become aware through experience, Tom and Edward must necessarily awaken to disenchantment and a perception of evil.

Tom is born into circumstances which prevent his fulfilling his natural gifts. He is restricted not only by poverty and brutishness, but by anti-intellectual public opinion. His sisters will not learn to read because they fear the jibes of their neighbors. Since Tom's real world is evil, he finds his freedom only in his dreams. He is not able to distinguish the dream and real worlds, and when he acts out his fancies, his parents and neighbors decide that he is mad.

Because Edward dreams of enjoying the free sports of normal boyhood, the exchange of identities grants both boys' wishes to be free of their encumbrances. Edward enters the unrestricted life of the commoner, and Tom realizes his romantic dreams. The switch is effected through a change of clothes, which gives Clemens an opportunity to illustrate his favorite political thesis, that attire is the only real indication of class distinction. The pair's paths diverge at this point, and although their separate adventures are quite different in detail, their meanings are ultimately the same: dreams are preferable to reality.

Tom's career as king is based on the pattern of the ragamuffin who becomes respectable only to find that his elevated station imposes terrible restraints. The pattern appears with variations in *Tom Sawyer* and *Huckleberry Finn*. Tom Canty seems at first to have achieved his desired freedom, for he is empowered to follow every whim. He puts this power to good use by following the dictates of his compassionate heart and his natural genius, settling criminal cases with incredible perspicacity and aplomb. Neither this legal aptitude nor his decision to end the Reign of Blood are prepared for, however, since until he begins to act officially he is only a frightened, romantic, miserable child. Clemens never indicates that Tom has generalized on the basis of his own condition and has fastened the blame for the commoner's misery on the King. In fact, he seems always to have accepted his misfortunes as his lot. However, Clemens means him to demonstrate his natural goodness at this point, and he does so, unbelievable as it may be.

Despite his opportunities for action, it is not long before Tom begins to chafe under the constant pressures of his new station. Courtly decorum bores him, and every duty and ritual obligation is a heavy burden. The narrator underscores Tom's growing disillusionment when he observes, "His old dreams had been so pleasant, but this reality was so dreary." Tom himself finally utters his despair: "In what way have I offended, that the good God should take me away from the fields and the free air . . . and make me a king and afflict me so?"[5] Thus the path from innocent illusion to disenchantment leads also from unsettled nature to populous and institutionalized society.

Edward's adventures also follow a familiar pattern. His tour through the kingdom is similar to the travels of the Pilgrim, the Greenhorn, and Huck Finn; and it is almost identical to Arthur's journey in *A Connecticut Yankee*. In *The Prince and the Pauper*, as in these other works, the innocent proceeds from ignorance to enlightenment as he travels through a wonderful countryside. This ethereal domain is a perfect example of the Innocent Land:

> All his sensations and experiences, as he moved through this solemn gloom and the empty vastness of the night, were new and strange to him. At intervals he heard voices approach, pass by, and fade into silence; and as he saw nothing more of the bodies they belonged to than a sort of formless drifting blur, there was something spectral and uncanny about it all that made him shudder. Occasionally he caught the twinkle of a light—always far away apparently—almost in another world; if he heard the tinkle of a sheep's bell, it was vague, distant, indistinct; the muffled lowing of the herds floated to him on the night wind in vanishing cadences, a mournful sound; now and then came the complaining howl of a dog over viewless expanses of field and forest; all sounds were remote; they made the little king feel that all life and activity were far removed from him, and that he stood solitary, companionless, in the center of a measureless solitude.[6]

Edward's emotions on this occasion are equally familiar. They recall those which Clemens described in *Roughing It* as he stood atop

Kilauea volcano in Hawaii, and they look forward to the sensations which accompany Theodor Fischer's awakening in *The Mysterious Stranger*.

Edward, like Huck, travels in disguise and obliterates his identity. The world in which he moves is new and strange to him, mainly because it is so much larger than the one he knows. The countryside is rural rather than urban, and any signs of human habitation seem to be in another world. The whole scene, in fact, is a great spectral garden. Like Huck and the Greenhorn, he encounters disembodied voices. All sensations are blurred, indistinct, and vague. The atmosphere is dreamlike. In a later passage, Clemens compares this expansive land to the sea: "It was a fair region, dotted with cottages and orchards, and the road led through broad pasture lands whose receding expanses, marked with gentle elevations and depressions, suggested the swelling and subsiding undulations of the sea."[7] While the land here is more of this world, with its homesteads and cultivated plots, the idyllic pastoral setting and its marine spaciousness remove it from reality.

Edward's moral journey begins in ignorant pride and ends in enlightened humility. When he acts like a king, the rogues mock him, and his guide, Miles Hendon, thinks he is mad. He suffers under his own laws, travels with thieves, goes hungry, and is tormented by a madman. At one point he is frightened, like "any other boy," and he gratefully accepts the final humiliation of sleeping with a calf.

Although both boys' adventures lead from happy illusion to disenchantment, the book's statement is not altogether negative. Tom relieves suffering and evil when he is empowered to impose his innocent will on the world. His good heart and his native genius are decidedly effective. Innocence, here, is a positive force and not just a state of self-deception. Moreover, Edward awakens to social awareness by suffering under his own laws. His enlightenment makes him a wiser and more humane monarch.

"The Private History of a Campaign that Failed" seems to be only coincidentally a story about innocence. Like *Roughing It, The Innocents Abroad,* and "Captain Stormfield," it concentrates on setting and situation and uses the innocent character to organize external details. Still, it tells of an innocent's progress from romantic illusion to awareness, and it indicates how conventional Clemens' treatment of the subject had become by 1884. The characterization, setting, and structure are similar to those in the rest of Clemens' stories of innocence, and these techniques seem to have come ready-made to the author's mind when he sat down to write his story.

The story suggests that Clemens originally intended it to be chiefly a local-color piece, describing the state of the Confederacy prior to its orderly mobilization for war. Clemens calls it "a picture of what went on in many and many a militia camp in the first months of the rebellion," [8] and the bulk of the material focuses on the Southern countryside, typical Southern people, and Southern attitudes toward the war. Second, it was apparently intended to highlight the folly and absurdity of war. The hero's education consists mainly in his realization that war is brutal, "the killing of strangers against whom you feel no personal animosity, strangers whom, in other circumstances, you would help if you found them in trouble, and who would help you if you needed it." [9] Third, the story implies a connection between the war and the Southern tendency toward romanticism and "nickel-plated aristocratic instincts," a charge that Clemens made often. The story, however, is somewhat ambiguous, since the apparent preference for innocent illusion that Clemens betrays in the narrative undermines the ostensible benefits of the recruit's experience and vitiates the attack on romanticism. The narrative method, characterization, and action all contribute to this impression of ambivalence.

As in "Old Times," the initiated hero tells the story of his own innocence. He speaks mostly as a reliable narrator, shifting only to the innocent persona to dramatize a characteristic opinion. For example, when the campaigners hear that a farmhouse nearby contains Union troops, the reliable narrator says, "It was a crucial moment; we realized with a cold suddenness that here was no jest—we were standing face to face with actual war." The narrator here is closely attuned to the emotions of the innocent, but he is still speaking in his own voice. Then he continues:

> We were equal to the occasion. In our response there was no
> hesitation, no indecision: we said that if Lyman wanted to meddle with

those soldiers he could go ahead and do it, but if he waited for us to
follow him, he would wait a long time.[10]

The phrases "equal to the occasion" and "no hesitation" are obviously inappropriate to the decision which follows. They are words
of resolute action, but the only action here is retreat. Since the
narrator indicates no awareness of the incongruity, he is now speaking from the innocent point of view, in order to dramatize the
situation and make it humorous. Containing both the innocent and
aware voices, the narrative continually underscores the movement
from innocence to awareness, which is the main action of the story.

The narrator characterizes the innocent hero by relating his actions and by describing those of his colleagues who are "fair sam-
ple[s] of the kind of stuff" he is made of. The youth has a distinctly
romantic bent, for he and his friends form the militia company in
secret meetings, much as Tom Sawyer gathers his robber band in
McDougal's Cave. "An innocent" names the group The Marion
Rangers, and none of the company finds fault with the name, although it implies an unwarranted intrepidity and grandeur. One of
the company is "young, ignorant, good-natured, well-meaning, triv-
ial, full of romance, and given to reading chivalric novels and singing forlorn love-ditties." Another finds "nothing serious in life,"
and the hero himself is incapable of thinking and "full of unreason-
ing joy" to be going to war.[11]

Since the innocent hero loses faith in his romantic "authorities,"
which tell him only the glories of war, and learns that it is really evil
and brutal, his progress may be called an initiation. That is, he moves
away from fantasy and illusion toward evil reality by learning the
ways of society. And since he learns that the love of war is foolish
and that war is hateful, his initiation seems desirable. However, as
long as the boys are innocent, they refuse to engage with the enemy
and retreat at every sign of possible danger, frolicking in the woods
and generally enjoying themselves. It is only after the contact with
evil has taught them the truth about war that some of them go on to
be real soldiers, daring spies, intrepid heroes, and corpses. The innocents' war is harmless, for they have no desire to kill or risk being
killed. Theirs is a fanciful war of romance and boyish make-believe;
the real war of their initiation is the evil one. Consequently, while

the awakening may seem desirable because it teaches the truth about war, it is undesirable because it begets killing in earnest. The implicit statement, again, is that innocence is fallacious, but benign; awareness is true but evil.

When the pressures of the situation force the band to kill a stranger who may not even have been an enemy, they learn what war is about and align themselves on one of two sides. Some remain to fight with the newly forming regiment under General Harris. Others, like the hero, decide that since war is not romantic make-believe but real evil, they want no part of it and leave the service.

At this point the narrative ends, raising the problem of structure, not only in "A Campaign that Failed" but in all the works discussed so far. The young soldier makes his choice between evil awareness and benign innocence, turns his back on reality—the war—and fades out of the picture. The situation is basically the same in the works which precede this story: the hero vanishes shortly after awakening to reality. One of two reasons accounts for his disappearance, depending on whether the action is initiatory or denitiatory. If the story recounts a denitiation, its purpose is to show the hero casting off his civilized predispositions and entering a free land of infinite possibility. When this decivilizing process is complete, therefore, the story ends and the hero stands disencumbered of his restrictions, ready to pursue his course of self-fulfillment. If, on the other hand, the hero is initiated, he awakes from his illusory ideas of a benign and orderly cosmos to a perception of evil and chaos. With nothing positive to rely on, he cannot act, so he moves off the scene in an atmosphere of nostalgia and deprivation. R. W. B. Lewis has said, "The imitation of an action (as Aristotle defined dramatic poetry) is an unrewarding undertaking whether life reveals too much good will or too much evil; for in the former case, action is unnecessary; in the latter it is impossible." [12] These two situations apply, I believe, to the denitiation and initiation, respectively, but the difficulties are more than just theoretical. Clemens could no more conceive and dramatize self-fulfillment, than he could reconcile himself to a reality which he saw as evil. His ideas of the freedom that denitiation brings are so vague and general that he never shows his emancipated hero using his new-found knowledge. Similarly, he saw little possibility for effective action in an evil universe, so initiation generally paralyzes his heroes.

These twin difficulties help establish the structure of all the stories of initiation and denitiation up through "A Campaign that Failed." The Pilgrim in *The Innocents Abroad* ceases to exist when travel and experience destroy his boyhood dreams. The Greenhorn in *Roughing It* and Captain Stormfield both disappear from the action when their emancipation from society is complete. Laura dies immediately after perceiving the hopelessness of her condition. Clemens drops Tom Sawyer's biography when it stops being the "history of a *boy*" and threatens to become "the history of a *man*." [13] The Cub's adventures end with his initiation into pilothood. *The Prince and the Pauper,* finally concludes with the awakening of the two heroes; despite the vaunted benefits of their initiation, Edward dies young, and only a brief paragraph is devoted to Tom's adult life.

It may be argued that since *The Innocents Abroad* is the chronicle of a pleasure trip, it closes with the end of that trip. Similarly, *Tom Sawyer* is a boy's story and closes properly with the advent of manhood, and Laura's case is that of the typical melodramatic *femme fatale* who is struck down by poetic justice. Tom and Edward have no reason to continue once the change in identities is cleared up, and "A Campaign that Failed" has fulfilled its aim to portray life in the Confederate Army before the war began in earnest. Still, Clemens drops the Greenhorn when *Roughing It* is only half completed, and Captain Stormfield never has a chance to apply his new knowledge toward any concrete ends. When Clemens incorporated "Old Times on the Mississippi" into *Life on the Mississippi* he made a desultory attempt to continue the young hero's adventures past the point where he gives up his innocent illusions about the river, but dropped him before the book was half finished. These latter cases suggest that the justifications for the truncated structure in the former examples may be fortuitous, and that their heroes might have vanished whether the external circumstances had warranted such conclusions or not. [14]

"Old Times on the Mississippi," *The Prince and the Pauper,* and "The Private History of a Campaign that Failed" illustrate Clemens' developing methods for handling the theme of initiation. All three stories describe the hero's passage from innocent illusion to awareness through a confrontation with evil. *The Prince and the Pauper* is Clemens' first attempt to make innocence and its adventures the center of the narrative. The three works bring to a conclusion the literary development of the theme which culminated in *Huckleberry Finn.*

5.

The Backwoods Angel

ADVENTURES OF
HUCKLEBERRY FINN

Iᴛ ᴄʟᴇᴍᴇɴꜱ' literary reputation rested solely on the works which precede *Huckleberry Finn,* it would be considerable. His ear for the native language, his control of tone, his ability to define an attitude by means of oral inflection, and what has been called his constitutional inability to write a flat sentence, require us to label him a major literary talent. But it is *Huckleberry Finn* alone that persuades us to elevate him above even that lofty rank and call him a genius, a prophet, "the Lincoln of our literature." As we look back over the work which culminates in Clemens' great book, we see him continually borrowing from his culture, metaphors, values, attitudes, settings, character-types, situations, and language. In *Huckleberry Finn,* he pays it all back tenfold, but in a currency that, through conversion, appeared so strange to his audience that they either refused to accept it or else took it for something other than what it so surely was—a statement of serious reservation about the ideals upon which Americans had erected their civilization.

The ideals of optimism, confidence, hope, divine purpose, individualism, and absolute freedom had been questioned before, by such members of the "devil's party" as Hawthorne, Melville, and Emily Dickinson. But Hawthorne and Melville leapt upon their culture from behind and above—from the forgotten convictions of Puritan theology and from the lofty and brooding peaks inhabited by Shakespeare and the Biblical Prophets. And Emily Dickinson waged her battle in secret and reserved her tale of death and doubt for her own ears. But Clemens rose directly out of the very culture he attacked, and he used its own weapons—its language and its dreams. If Hawthorne and Melville saw further ahead sooner, it was because they stood on higher ground. Clemens was the first to see from the plain that our professed beliefs and our actions were tragically incompatible.

The sharpness of Clemens' vision we may ascribe to his tendency to think in concrete metaphors, rather than in abstractions. Henry Nash Smith has said that he was a presentational thinker, incapable of sustained logical speculation.[1] This judgment needs no further proof than a comparison of the strengths of his fiction and the embarrassing weaknesses of his "philosophical" essays. The habit of presentational thought distinguishes, very often, the writer of fiction from the philosopher and the essayist. Usually, the true novelist—like the true poet—cannot be asked to state his views in terms other than those of action, character, and setting. Unlike the critic, he resists on principle the temptation to distinguish between what his work says and what it "means." There is a sense in which we may call the inability to sustain abstract discourse, a deficiency, a failure of intellect, discipline, and training. But in another sense, it may appear as a blessing, particularly when it is supplanted by the literary gift of metaphorical thought. In Clemens' case, had he felt more at home with the methods of discursive reason, we might know him today as a popular spokesman of nineteenth-century American attitudes. We cannot imagine that he would ever have become such a fearless and creative philosopher that he could have risen much above the heavy demands his audience made on him. As it stands, his essays abound in popular delusions, clichés, and general muddleheadedness. And the fault does not lie entirely with his society, for he was often much in agreement with his time. He was as willing to censor his own antisocial impulses as he was to acquiesce in the guidance of his wife or his editor.

The case seems to be, rather, that when he could create characters in whom he could invest his deepest longings, and then place them in a setting which he knew from instinct and experience, these characters would work out their destinies according to an inner necessity, free from the censorious meddling of *both* Clemens and his advisors. His fiction—particularly in his years of doubt and anxiety—could often arrive at conclusions which he could not otherwise articulate. Few characters in our fiction seem so completely autonomous as Huck Finn. He behaves as he does because his character and his situation demand it. Placed, as he is, in a world of the author's imagining, the boy comes alive in the way that distinguishes the great figures of fiction from the gangling puppets of less accomplished writers. Except for the very necessary convictions of the author which define the moral cosmos in which Huck must operate, there are no strings on him. As we follow him through the first chapters of his adventures, our attention never strays from him to an author who keeps adjusting the action to meet with some previously conceived requirement.

Writing of this sort is truly "creative," for it becomes a process of understanding a problem in its own terms, rather than according to some pre-existent formula. Furthermore, it can hold as many surprises for the author as for the audience. As we have already seen, Clemens was dismayed by the way Tom Sawyer "turned out." He was even more deeply disturbed by the direction which Huck eventually took. Although we have no explicit evidence of Clemens' concern with the outcome of *Huckleberry Finn*—as we do in the case of *Tom Sawyer*—the evasion sequence of the last ten chapters seems to represent the author's conscious intrusion into the action, to forestall the conclusions toward which Huck's adventures were inevitably heading. Clemens seems to have stepped in at this point to avoid having to face certain truths about his hero—not simply because they violated social ideals, but because they attacked the very foundations of his own professed faith. But, while the novel suffers seriously from the terrible inappropriateness of that final episode, it still achieves thematic consistency. The very nature of the evasion points up the hard truth of the earlier chapters and confirms—in its own clumsy, rambling fashion—the dark vision Clemens tried to avoid.

In the preceding chapters we have seen Clemens experimenting with the character of the innocent—developing his voice; defining his traits of innate goodness, natural sagacity, love of freedom, and fear of restraint; and assaying his chances for beneficent growth. We have seen him working out the two possible courses of action the innocent may follow: from freedom and happy ignorance to restraint and care, and from bothersome social routine to expanded possibility and compassion. And, we have seen him collecting the details of setting which become, for him, increasingly symbolic through repeated use. In *Huckleberry Finn,* Clemens employs these fictive metaphors of character, action, and setting, to test the viability of the ideals of progress, optimism, human goodness, freedom, and individualism, which he shared with his culture. The novel examines in complex detail the conflicting principles of freedom and authority, experience and tradition, instinct and reason, nature and civilization, through the story of a boy's struggle against meddlers who seek to control him. All of these conflicts appear as adjuncts to the novel's central problem: the fight between the individual and society.

The idea of innocence can clarify the meaning of this struggle which is the core of the novel. Fundamentally, the book states that individual man is innocent and that social man is corrupt. The action of the story concerns the innocent's confronting an evil society and his solution of the problems which the confrontation raises. The novel takes its form from this theme and action, and its success depends largely on the author's ability to solve the central problem of the individual's relation to society. Furthermore, both the narrative mode, which arises ultimately out of the tradition of American humor, and the central theme are inextricably linked to the question of innocence.

The innocent, as I have defined him, is an amalgamation of the vernacular backwoodsman of the old frame-story, and the romantically inclined voyager of literary travel-burlesque. The dominant trait he derives from both traditions is his tendency to see only the appearance of life, to speak in a voice that is unconsciously ironic. This voice endeared him to Clemens as a perfect medium for satire, and he functions in this capacity throughout the works I have discussed so far. Early in the innocent's career, however, he began to transcend his limitations as an "inspired idiot" who comments on reality by describing appearances; in *The Innocents Abroad* he already possesses some of the non-ironic qualities which make him a symbol of sinless youth, happy ignorance, freedom, and absence of care. In the course of his development, moreover, these symbolic traits gradually take precedence over his inspired idiocy. Although his innocence remains secondary to his ironic viewpoint and the surroundings upon which he comments in *Roughing It,* "Captain Stormfield," "Old Times on the Mississippi," and "A Campaign that Failed," his importance as a distinct character-type with a peculiar adventure of its own is increasingly evident in these works, and especially in *The Gilded Age, The Prince and the Pauper,* and *Tom Sawyer.* In these last three books he begins as a satirical voice but very soon develops aspirations and passions which separate him from the satirical theme, even to the extent that he contradicts that theme in *Tom Sawyer* and *The Gilded Age.* Clemens' problem all along, it seems, was to make the two forces work together instead of at cross-purposes. *Huckleberry Finn* stands above all the rest of Clemens' work because it achieves the greatest degree of cooperation between the theme and the innocent hero.

In the course of his gradual definition, the innocent acquires certain accessory characteristics, which he exhibits in all subsequent appearances. He is generally devoid of social or family background, as in *The Innocents Abroad* and *Roughing It,* and Clemens very often makes him an orphan. In addition, he is good-hearted and compassionate, and the depth of his immersion in civilized society usually determines how much he can obey his charitable impulses. Consequently, he manifests an inborn urge to be free of all sorts of external restraints and pressure, and devotes much of his energy to this end. Finally, he is close to nature, for that is the source of his energy and of his most endearing traits. As long as he retains his innocence he allies himself with nature against civilization.

The adventure of this innocent invariably has to do with an educational process which may take one of two basic forms: an initiation into society or a denitiation away from it. In either case, he spends some part of his existence in an idyllic setting which symbol-

izes freedom, repose, and infinite possibility. If the action is denitiatory, he enters this magic land as he leaves society behind. If his
story involves an initiation, he leaves the Innocent Land as he learns
that freedom is a dream and that evil constraint is the only reality.
Both of these patterns of action, it is plain, depend upon a conflict
between the individual, who is free and innocent, and society, which
is restrictive and evil.

These two types of education assert what is "real." The key to
reality in each is what Clemens calls the "authorities." When the
hero moves away from society, the authorities are social prejudices.
When he is initiated into civilization, they are his childish illusions.
In both situations, the hero loses faith in his illusory authorities and
perceives "reality," which is freedom in the denitiation and evil
constraint in the initiation. In addition, the innocent who is to be
initiated places his faith in romantic fiction, a literary genre for
which Clemens had little respect. Although Clemens suggests that
goodness and freedom are unreal by depicting them as literary lies in
his works on initiation, he generally makes the initiated hero look
back with longing to his false dreams, preferring them to evil reality.

Among the several remarkable achievements of *Huckleberry Finn*,
perhaps the most notable is its combination of the first-person point
of view and the vernacular idiom.[2] Surely this technique is responsible for the greatest strengths and, paradoxically, some of the most
glaring weaknesses of the novel. What prompted Clemens to let Huck
tell his own story in his own language?

In discussing *Tom Sawyer*, I suggested that Clemens was dissat-
isfied with the book because Tom turns out to be a respectable adult,
a solid citizen, and "an ordinary liar." This unfortunate turn of
events rose out of Clemens' desire to tell the story of a bad boy who
makes good, in the socially acceptable sense. In other words, the
adult, non-innocent, detached point of view virtually destroys the
innocence which a sympathetic point of view created. In his letter to
Howells regarding *Tom Sawyer* and its projected sequel, Clemens
says that he will take a boy and run him through life in the first
person, but that he will not use Tom. Even at this early stage in the

book's history Clemens' dominant impulse seems to have been to identify himself as completely as possible with his innocent hero, to let him tell his own story without the corrupting influence of the adult, who has satirical aims not in keeping with the sanctity of innocence.

This is the crucial point, I believe, at which satire and innocence finally strike a balance. The difference between Tom in his book and Huck in his is very much like that between Laura and Colonel Sellers in *The Gilded Age*. Although Laura may have been conceived as an instrument of satire, Clemens is so sympathetic to her innocent nature that she is all sentiment and no satire. Conversely, although Sellers possesses many innocent traits—especially good-heartedness —he remains a buffoon for most of the book. The difference is that Clemens identifies with Laura and retains an almost constant comic detachment from Sellers. By the time he wrote *Tom Sawyer*, Clemens had apparently learned to restrain his most sentimental tendencies, so the passages in which he identifies with Tom escape the sickening pathos which characterizes Laura's history; but his detachment from his hero at certain points in the novel still lowers the boy to the level of a fool. In *Huckleberry Finn*, however, he manages to identify himself with his hero, for the most part, without sentimentalizing; and by always looking at the world from within Huck instead of looking at him from the outside, he avoids the danger of abusing his hero.

The first-person point of view had one further attraction for Clemens. By selecting a narrator who is less intelligent than himself, he relieves himself of the responsibility of defining explicitly certain problems which would occur to his adult mind but not to the limited intelligence of an adolescent boy. Although the first-person mode enables him to comment on society with considerable ironic force, it also narrows the scope of his awareness and the range of his logical statement. There is little doubt that he imposed this limitation upon himself because he was unable to explain the incomprehensible forces which were restricting and annoying him with greater malignity every year. His whole intellectual biography is a procession of personal disenchantments, bitter renunciations, confused gropings among quack sciences for pat systems, and weak philosophies. When he retired into Huck's mind, he regressed into a world he could understand, a world he longed for with embarrassing regularity throughout his adult life.

The first-person point of view, then, is the logical conclusion to a development that began as far back as the Snodgrass letters. In that work, and later in "The Jumping Frog" and "Captain Stormfield," Clemens explored the possibility of effacing himself entirely from his narrative, leaving the vernacular speaker to describe appearances with his characteristic lack of humor and to suggest the reality, thereby creating unconscious irony. In those earlier works Clemens' primary impulse for using the unreliable narrator seems to have been the humorous possibilities that the method raised; and although "Captain Stormfield" does avoid some philosophical problems by being narrated by an ignorant old sailor, Clemens' need for such an escape does not become evident until *Tom Sawyer*. The works which immediately precede *Huckleberry Finn* and all of those which follow it strongly indicate Clemens' desire to turn back to a time when the world was, supposedly, understandable, to avoid the onerous task of creating a meaningful reality as a basis for action and irony.

Although the point of view and the vernacular style limit the intellectual range of the book, they make possible some of its most considerable merits. As so many critics have noted, Huck's language gives Clemens a new depth of perception, a fresh stock of descriptive techniques, a stylistic vigor, and a tremendous release of imaginative power. And what is most important, the narrative mode and the style enabled Clemens to see his innocent hero steadily for the greatest part of the book, to make Huck the vehicle of the satire without making him the butt of the jokes. Even the final episode, in which Clemens loses the close attachment to Huck that the point of view originally gave him, cannot entirely erase the superb achievement of those chapters in which the author, character, and language are working together.

Just as Clemens' ideas on innocence determine the point of view and language of *Huckleberry Finn,* they also define the central problem of the novel, the struggle between innocent natural man and depraved civilization. The concept that man is naturally good and only becomes corrupt as he succumbs to the pressures of civilized institutions is certainly not new with Clemens, and it is subject to the same criticisms that have been leveled against similar philosophies. The most obvious of these objections, and also the most devastating, argues that if man were good, evil institutions would not exist, since institutions are man-made. Clemens never solves this problem, nor is there any definite indication that the objection ever occurred to him. Instead he stoutly maintains throughout the novel that a man is good as long as he exists in a natural setting and continually evades the corrupting pressures and influences of civilization. Because the novel fails to solve the problem of man *versus* society, Huck turns out to be a largely theoretical case. He illustrates what a man *would* be like if he were not civilized, but he offers little positive help for the man who recognizes his social role and seeks a way to make his situation meaningful.

In keeping with the negative tone of the theme, the dominant action of the novel is a series of evasions. Moreover, the motivating force behind each of the several evasive courses which Huck takes is social evil itself. Whenever civilized decorum, viciousness, or restraint touches him, he tries to escape; he is at rest only so long as external pressures leave him alone. Evil, in fact, is the only positive force in the book; goodness survives not through conflict and victory but only by running away. This pervasiveness of evil, moreover, foreshadows the direction of the final chapters. This episode, as I hope to show, is Clemens' substitution for a conclusion that the theme demands but which he could not bring himself to set down.

Since the action is predominantly evasive, it is fitting that the structure be mainly denitiatory. Huck's quest for freedom, which drives him out of St. Petersburg and down the river to the Phelps farm, leads him away from society. Like the Greenhorn and Captain Stormfield, he moves away from society into an Innocent Land in which he can exercise his natural benevolence and compassion. But Huck's story is far more complex than that of *Roughing It* or "Captain Stormfield," for while he leaves society behind in St. Petersburg, he encounters it again and again as he moves downstream. This new development in the denitiation structure seems to be the result of two related difficulties. First, Clemens was faced with the problem of providing motivation for Huck's movement comparable with the Greenhorn's job in Carson City and the Captain's death. Second, since Huck's journey, unlike the preceding two, would not deliver him geographically from civilization, and since his original impulse to flee had come from the oppressions and dangers of life in St. Petersburg, Clemens renews the impulse whenever necessary by having Huck confront similar evils on his way South. Consequently, Huck's adventure, although basically denitiatory, is overlaid with a set of experiences which acquaint him even more fully with the evil of society. In other words, the experience is denitiatory and initiatory at the same time.

Furthermore, the evasive tenor of the action defines Huck's relationship to that action and, consequently, indicates a change in Clemens' opinions on the efficacy of innocence since he wrote *The Prince and the Pauper*. Except when, motivated by his sentimental attachment to Miss Mary Jane, he hides Peter Wilks' gold, Huck never really engages in the panorama of activity along the river. He is generally the victim of forces that are beyond his control because they are alien to his innocent nature. He is passive, detached—an observer rather than an effectual agent. While it remains a positive value, innocence in *Huckleberry Finn* has no power, as it did in *The Prince and the Pauper,* to right social evil. Instead it is victimized, and Huck's main response to evil aggression is flight. Not only has Clemens lost any sense he might have had of innocence vitalized through a confrontation with evil, he has become disenchanted with the power of innocence to combat evil. There is no longer any evidence in Clemens' work that innocence can survive in an evil world; its continuance depends almost entirely on complete separation from civilization.

In the opening chapters of the book Huck is on his way to the respectable fate which entraps Tom at the end of *Tom Sawyer*. But he has already shown in that earlier work an instinctual desire for freedom and a canny suspicion of institutions, which now cause him to chafe under the regularity of the Widow Douglas' routines. Consequently, it is not long before he runs away again, only to be brought back once more by Tom, that arch-defector from innocence, who now substitutes the stuff of romantic fiction for the genuine boons of innocent freedom that he once enjoyed. But Huck's instincts prevail, and Tom's tawdry fancies offer him no respite from the Widow's infringements on his freedom. Neither the robber-band, with its chivalrous codes of courtly love and revenge, nor the raid on the Sunday-school picnic satisfies Huck's indomitable urge to be off.

St. Petersburg society furnishes a microcosmic picture of the evils which the world launches against innocence. Clothes, those badges of lost innocence, torment Huck with their stiffness and "smotheriness." School and Sunday school demand his attention and curb his mobility. The conflicting dogmas of Miss Watson's and the Widow Douglas' religions confuse him, leaving him with little more than an impression of the equal senselessness of all dogma. Pap's mercurial rise and fall clearly demonstrate society's inability to right its own wrongs, suggesting that ingrained depravity is irremediable. Huck's new fortune, the main instrument of his rise to social acceptance, only brings him trouble from Pap, so he gives it away to Judge Thatcher. Pap's squabbles with the Judge over the custody of Huck increase the boy's anxieties. Although Huck never fully realizes it, his primary difficulty rests on this question, for what he wants is to have custody over himself, not to be delivered into the hands of either the "best" or the "worst" man in town.

Tom represents many of the social attitudes which Huck will have to unlearn during his flight down the river. When Tom finds Jim asleep, he hangs the slave's hat on a tree to convince him that he has been ridden by witches; but Huck will discover on the raft the error of tormenting his companion. Tom advocates the vendetta in the *code duello* of the robber-band; but Huck will see the waste of this barbarous ethic in action at the Grangerford plantation. The romance of robbery and murder, which Tom champions, will vanish in the face of terrible reality aboard the *Walter Scott*, and along with it Huck's slight faith in the bookish "authorities" which Tom espouses.

Pap sums up the accumulating themes of civilized depravity in a thundering coda when he rants drunkenly against the injustices which he fancies have been perpetrated against him. Having kidnapped Huck, he locks him in the cabin and declaims against the government, free Negroes, and the respectable citizens of St. Petersburg, completing the list he began when he first appeared in Huck's room at the Widow's and attacked learning, families, tradition, and religion. The scene closes with the old man in delirious flight from the Death Angel and Huck ensconced in a corner, prepared to kill his father to protect himself from destruction.

Throughout these introductory episodes Huck continually displays the instinctive urge to be free. This natural drive proclaims his innocence and appears to be a positive force in opposition to evil. The will to freedom displays itself only as a response to external stimulus, however, and not as an efficient cause of action. Innocence is a state of repose and inertia; suggesting satisfaction, it requires no action. Consequently, only society's invasion of the innocent's freedom causes him to act. As long as innocence prevails, no activity is necessary; but when evil threatens, innocence must react. Insofar as only those forces which beleaguer innocence motivate action, the moral cosmos in which that action takes place remains predominantly malicious. Innocence appears largely in relief, isolated and defined by encircling ill will.

Goaded by social evil which threatens his freedom, Huck embarks upon the river—the Innocent Land—seeking refuge in this idyllic setting of mystery and repose. After escaping from Pap's cabin, he falls asleep in the canoe. When he awakes, he pulls out into the river, away from the real world, and a view of Pap, the epitome of everything he is leaving behind, marks the transition. Out in the stream he describes the scenery in a dreamlike passage, which employs the conventions Clemens has developed in the many previous descriptions of the Innocent Land. The physical limitations of space open up for Huck as he sets out. The sky seems "ever so deep" as he lies on his back in the canoe. The river appears "miles and miles across," but he can see over great distances and count the drift logs "hundreds of yards out from shore." He can hear mysterious, disembodied voices coming to him from "a long way off," and the voice of a distant raftsman is as clear to him as if the man were by his side.[3] These confused distances, heightened sensory powers, receding spatial boundaries, and dreamlike appearances recall similar descriptions in *Roughing It*, "Captain Stormfield," and *Tom Sawyer*.

72

Magic abounds in the Delectable Land in the form of superstition. Although the searchers on the steamboat cannot see Huck, who remains "invisible" in his hiding place on Jackson's Island, the bread that has been set out finds him. Jim's warnings about the folly of playing with snake-skins prove terribly true before the journey ends, and his prognostications based on his "dream" of the raft in the fog and on his "hairy breas' " are fulfilled almost without exception. Superstition and magic not only create a fantastic atmosphere for the Innocent Land, but they indicate Huck's predominantly melancholy temperament, and foreshadow disasters to come.

The Innocent Land is also an idyllic setting, in which the innocent communes with nature. On Jackson's Island a squirrel jabbers at Huck "very friendly." Huck is at home and comfortable in a terrific storm, and after the sky clears he goes out in the canoe to visit stranded animals, who are not afraid of him. On the raft he and Jim contemplate the stars, and he revels in the beauties of a sunrise. At home in nature, he and Jim shed their clothing and go naked, as Clemens' innocents so often do in their proper environment.

Just as Tom represents so many aspects of the civilized world, Jim embodies the virtues and esoteric knowledge of the Innocent Land. Whenever Tom is in control of the action, in St. Peterburg or on the Phelps farm, Jim is a buffoon and a simpleton. But on the river the superstitious, wily Negro is in his element. He guides Huck through the river world, interpreting its signs and portents, instructing his young companion in its mysteries. At home, he shares Huck's fate, for he, too, is a fugitive from society. He and Huck are both born outcasts whose social position depends on their monetary worth; and both are victims of a civilized lust for money. Furthermore, Jim's status as a slave is the palpable symbol of the constraint Huck is fleeing, and slavery epitomizes the civilized institutions which Clemens attacks in the novel.

Because Jim shares so many of Huck's misfortunes and because he represents the fugitive freedom of the Innocent Land, he is the proper object of Huck's moral speculations. As a Negro, Jim can measure the Southern white boy's increasing detachment from institutionalized society and his expanding natural benevolence. In Jim's world Huck slowly learns to treat his companion as a human being, even though he never sufficiently abstracts his feelings for Jim to apply them to Negroes or slavery in general.

Once Huck and Jim are out of St. Petersburg and together in the Innocent Land, where their finer instincts and natural dignity have room to fulfill themselves, the problem of continued movement and meaningful action arises. The flow of the river and the passivity of the raft provide a means of locomotion, but the inexorable drift southward makes Jim's quest for freedom a mockery. Clemens obviously wanted to send Huck and Jim together through the river world and to have Huck develop his humane instincts in that setting, but the geographical facts of setting created difficulties that had to be solved. Walter Blair discusses these problems and their solution, so they need not be rehearsed here.[4] The important point is that Clemens revised his earlier version of the story to enable Huck and Jim to continue their journey, the meaning of which was clearly more important to him than the realistic inconsistencies.

The essential details of the journey must show innocent man in conflict with corrupt society, and Clemens develops his theme by having Huck make periodic forays into civilization along the river. These repeated confrontations have two results, similar in effect and meaning: they motivate continued movement downstream by threatening the innocent pair with coercion and destruction, and they show how impotent innocence is when evil attacks it. Only by running away, by continuing the evasive action that characterizes the entire novel, can Huck and Jim retain the freedom upon which their innocence depends. In addition, these episodes, which I have already called initiatory, further acquaint Huck with the baseness of society and gradually develop in him the emotional state upon which he bases his final decision to go to hell rather than betray Jim.

The first of these episodes, the adventure in the House of Death, pertains to the action and meaning of the novel in three ways. First, the house supplies Huck and Jim with tools and clothing, which they will use throughout their journey—especially the clothing, with which Huck disguises himself as a girl and Jim as a sick Arab. Second, Jim decides not to tell Huck that the dead man in the house is Pap in order to spare his young friend the horror of seeing his

74

father dead from a bullet wound. Pap must die so that Huck can decide freely about returning to society at the end of the book. But by withholding this information Jim justifies Huck's continued flight, for the boy could stop running if he knew that his most annoying and dangerous adversary was dead. Third, the house is a bit of civilization ripped from the world Huck and Jim have left behind, and it is the very image of civilized degeneracy. The revulsion that Huck feels on viewing this sight, set against the obvious affection he already feels for Jim, prepares him for his ultimate choice between loyalty to his friend and civilized respectability.

The two adventures which follow, Huck's visit to Mrs. Loftus' and the boarding of the *Walter Scott,* have similarly complex significances. In the former episode Huck learns that a posse is after Jim, and that they must continue their flight. Although the men are looking only for Jim, Huck says, "They're after *us,*" evidencing his growing association with the slave against society. Also, Mrs. Loftus, sympathetic and kind-hearted as she is, displays the civilized prejudices of white society when she assumes that Jim is Huck's killer even though Huck has been very careful to implicate Pap. The *Walter Scott,* like the House of Death, supplies Huck with useful articles: the history books which prepare him to discuss royalty with Jim and to evaluate the King and the Duke. Even more important, Huck learns what Tom's romantic ideas of robbery and murder are like when they are put into actual practice. The name Walter Scott is particularly appropriate here, for as the symbol of sentimental romance sinks, Huck refuses to sentimentalize over the unavoidable death of the robbers. Huck is willing to accept responsibility for his actions, as is shown by the guilt he feels after Jim is bitten by the snake; but he sensibly declines to affect remorse over conditions beyond his control. Again, Huck's experiences disenchant him with civilized conventions and social prejudices and bind him more closely to Jim and to the Innocent World.

Clemens carefully constructs the next incident, Huck's stay at the Grangerfords, giving him time to become close to the family so that their eventual destruction can touch him more deeply than did the deaths of the robbers on the *Walter Scott.* The fate of Packard, Bill, and Turner acquaints Huck with the folly of violence and crime, but

75

through a close, personal attachment to a large, healthy family he can appreciate their terrible waste.[5] Admirable as the feuding Shepherdsons and Grangerfords may be in many respects, they are finally just a pack of aging Tom Sawyers, whose adherence to an outworn code of ethics has only produced a long roster of honored dead. Tom's story-book conduct is not only impractical and silly, as Huck thought in St. Petersburg, but destructive and criminal.

So far, innocence has survived only by running away from evil society, and now the invasion of the raft by the Duke and the King underscores its vulnerability. The raft is essentially passive, as I said before, lacking its own means of locomotion; and this impotence corresponds to the helplessness of its occupants.[6] Huck comments several times on the virtues of their refuge; for example, he remarks, "There warn't no home like a raft after all. Other places seem so cramped up and smothery, but a raft don't. You feel mighty free and easy and comfortable on a raft."[7] The two frauds even gain access to the raft by means of Huck's innocence, for he offers them help out of his natural compassion. They immediately take over, using Huck and Jim to further their own predatory schemes; and, significantly, they make Jim a slave again, drawing up a poster which labels him a runaway. They also paint him blue and call him a sick Arab. The two rogues bring discord to the raft for the first time, shattering the restful concord that Huck and Jim have enjoyed since setting out. In sum, they deprive the two fugitives of the serenity, freedom, and nobility that the Innocent Land has made possible.

The King and the Duke are masters at working the crowd, and by including Huck in their fraudulent enterprises, they introduce him to some of the characteristics man displays when he joins a group. The frantic worshippers at the tent revival, the audience at the "Royal Nonesuch," the calloused spectators at Bogg's shooting who form into a lynching mob only to be turned away by one brave man, the weeping mourners at the Wilks funeral, the mindless fun-seekers at the circus, and finally the vigilantes who torture the two rascals themselves, create a shocking panorama of civilized mankind. Huck generally manages to stay aloof from the mob, and he views each one from a detached position, never partaking in whatever insanity happens to be driving it. He joins the lynching party, but only as a spectator, and this is as close as he ever comes to being swallowed up by organized society in these episodes. Somehow, his reticence keeps him from sympathizing with any group; and by remaining a passive and ineffectual observer he preserves his submerged but inextinguishable innocence.

Huck faces his supreme test, the fearful decision to stick by Jim and take his chances with the devil, after a long series of experiences which have prepared his heart to make the correct choice. Besides the situations I have already outlined, which unfailingly prove the depravity of society and the desirability of individual innocence, there are a number of other incidents which determine Huck's choice. On the one side, Huck becomes increasingly aware of Jim's humanity. He learns humility in asking forgiveness for playing a thoughtless prank on his friend. He discovers that Jim is capable of human emotions when the Negro longs for his family and chastizes himself for treating his daughter unjustly. But then, every Negro in the novel is loyal. The Grangerfords' servant brings Huck and Jim together in the swamp, and a Negro saves the King from an angry mob. Huck grows to appreciate Jim's favors, rather than accepting them as services due from a slave. Also, Huck becomes a slave himself when the King makes him wait on tables with the Negroes. All of these situations help illuminate the heavy irony of Huck's statement, uttered after the Duke and the King have performed a particularly base act: "Well, if I ever struck anything like it, I'm a nigger. It was enough to make a body ashamed of the human race." [8]

On the other side of Huck's experience are his encounters with civilized men. People often refuse to help him when there is no profit in it for them. The ferry watchman is eager to save Huck's fictitious family when he believes that a reward is forthcoming. The men who are looking for the runaway slaves refuse, fortunately, to help Huck's "father," who is supposedly stricken with smallpox; and when Huck asks a fisherman for the name of a town, he gets only threats for an answer. The King and the Duke give him a particularly vivid impression of the depths to which civilized men will sink, and they also exemplify the fragility of a friendship based on mutual

gain rather than on sacrifice and esteem. Huck's awareness of civilized meanness receives its final stamp, of course, when the two
charlatans sell Jim for ''forty dirty dollars.''

By the time that Huck's conscience goads him into writing the
letter to Miss Watson, then, the opposing forces of society and of
innocence have aligned themselves for the moral battle. On one side
stand all of Huck's experiences, which have impressed his good heart
with the baseness of society and the goodness of his friend. On the
other are the civilized ideas which fill his head. Like Captain Stormfield, Huck has his prejudices in his head; there are none in his heart.
No mere penchant for irony prompted Clemens to have Huck conduct his self-examination entirely in society's terms or to state his
final resolution in words which imply his continued belief in institutionalized religion. When he argues logically, he uses his head and
employs the vocabulary of the schools and churches. But his final
decision comes from his heart, although he still phrases it in the
language of society. Back in St. Petersburg, under the tutelage of
Miss Watson and the Widow Douglas, Huck could never have arrived at his conclusion. But here in the Innocent World he casts off
the stifling ideas in his head—just as he sheds his clothes. His
decision to stand by Jim is one more evasion insofar as it renounces
society. No compromise between the good heart and the evil head is
possible.

It will not be necessary for me to discuss the weaknesses of the last
ten chapters beyond noticing that they mark the end of the journey
in the Innocent Land and, consequently, the cessation of most of the
noble traits which Huck and Jim have displayed there. It is Tom's
world again; Huck fades into the background, powerless to resist his
friend's romantic schemes. Jim, out of his proper element now,
reassumes his role as a comic butt. The task that remains to this
chapter is to explain some probable reasons for this much discussed ''falling off.''

Innocence throughout the book remains a secondary power at best,
a state which takes its shape from surrounding evil. It is extremely
vulnerable, and it exists only as long as it can avoid evil. In the
Innocent Land of freedom and repose Huck can act in accordance
with his instincts, but even there only negative actions are open to

him. Innocence requires activity only when evil threatens, otherwise it is a state of repose and inertia, and even then the only activity required or possible is evasion. Huck's resolution is largely negative: he decides *not* to betray Jim. Still, this state of "nonbeing" is preferable to evil, for society prohibits the decision not to be evil.

I believe that Clemens held this notion before he ever began the novel. *The Gilded Age* certainly gives sufficient evidence of such dualism. Furthermore, I believe that his obsessive desire to enter the Innocent World and to escape evil reality led him to look at the action of the book through the eyes of his innocent hero. Once he made this step he virtually abandoned all hope of reconciling the polar forces which constitute its theme. He had already decided to keep his hero innocent, as my analyses of *Tom Sawyer* and *The Gilded Age* indicate; and with such a goal in mind he could effect no satisfactory compromise. His previous attempts to initiate his innocents were, to him, failures; so Huck ends as he began, in flight. Significantly, he flees to "the Territory," the Innocent Land already explored with some degree of success in *Roughing It*. Theoretically, I suppose, the book should conclude with Huck's either employing his knowledge in some meaningful way or accepting the tragedy of his inability to do so. But Clemens' own biography reveals no indication that he ever found a place for innocence in society or that he could face the tragedy of lost innocence.

These final chapters do fail to solve the problems and reconcile the conflicts laid down in the heart of the novel. They violate the reader's expectations by dissipating into a kind of irresponsible foolery the seriousness with which he has come to regard Huck and his plight. For these reasons they betray in Clemens what Leo Marx calls "a failure of nerve." [9] But if we look beyond formal considerations to the cultural context of the novel, we detect a thematic consistency in the book which lends to the evasion scene a pathetic seriousness and considerable prophetic insight. Huck's task—to obey his decent impulses in an environment which is constitutionally opposed to natural decency—was Clemens' task as well. He spent his mature years trying to make the facts of his experience jibe with his ideals and his expectations. What is more, this conflict between fact and desire has been the most pressing spiritual issue in American culture since the first settlers tried to bring the finite capabilities of mortal men into line with the infinite will of God by erecting a society based on divine commandment.

Early in the novel Huck stands outside society, naturally suspicious of its restraints and hypocrisy, but largely convinced of its rightness and of his own depravity. When he fails to respond willingly to its mandates, he automatically assumes that he, not society, is imperfect; he has not been "brung up to it." When he refuses to surrender Jim, he is sure that he has willfully disobeyed a perfectly just moral commandment and that he will be duly punished. The irony of these episodes is obvious; Clemens clearly intends to expose the wickedness of a society which can make a humane act seem sinful. But he himself was not sufficiently emancipated to regard similar conflicts without uncertainty. Like Huck, he was deeply suspicious of social morality, but he craved public acceptance. Like Huck, he heard the promptings of an inner voice which advocated antisocial behavior, but the issues were not as clear in his own life as they were in his hero's. In *Huckleberry Finn,* the problem is reasonably simple: Huck's deepest urges lead him to acts which are absolutely good, while his social conscience inculcates values which are undeniably bad. The source and substance of each command is perfectly clear, to Clemens and the reader, and the choice is axiomatic. But in Clemens' own life, the two sides of the issue were not so clearly defined, and the rightness of the inner voice was not so self-evident. Clemens may have been on top of Huck's experience, but he was as confused as Huck by his own.

Evidence of this confusion appears everywhere in Clemens' life, but nowhere so clearly as in the terrible episode of the Whittier birthday dinner in 1877.[10] The invitation to address the assembled dinosaurs of American letters on that occasion signified acceptance, the stamp of respectability. Like Huck's money, we may assume, Clemens' success made him an object of concern to the establishment. But while Huck and his creator may have felt a degree of ingrained reverence for properly instituted powers, they were fundamentally hostile to them. In his heart, Clemens regarded any institution as opposed to change by the individual. Groups of individuals, he seems to have argued, erect institutions for their common benefit, only to find that these institutions restrict the very freedoms they were created to insure. So, while he rejoiced in his acceptance into respectable circles, he could not resist the temptation to ridicule these literary idols for their complacency and pretension.

In the speech itself, Clemens followed his usual practice of maintaining a reverent attitude while speaking in his own voice and then abusing the objects of reverence in the guise of a barbarous rustic— as he did in a speech before the Plymouth Society in 1881,[11] when he praised the founding fathers in his own voice and then attacked them viciously after assuming the rhetorical mask of a "border ruffian." But this device was lost on the audience at the Whittier dinner, who heard only the coarse drollery which he heaped upon them and their work. The yarn which makes up most of the talk is one of the funniest he ever wrote, and one of the most devastating, but the frosty silence which greeted it convinced Clemens that he had made a ghastly mistake. At this point he was faced with a crucial choice—not only on a question of taste, but of morals as well. He *knew* the talk was funny, and he confirmed this belief when he re-examined the speech years later. Yet he also knew that it was not acceptable. Like Huck, he could have said, "All right, then, I'll go to hell," and left Whittier, Longfellow, and Emerson to their sacrosanct delusions. But the inner voice was not strong enough. He accepted the judgment of Howells and others—indeed he magnified this judgment— and underwent an ordeal of guilty remorse he never forgot.

This decision, too, we might call "a failure of nerve"; but it is more accurately called, I think, a failure of faith—faith in the individual ability to discover a source of moral value. On this occasion, I believe, Clemens retained the desire to rely on his personal judgment, but lost the confidence that enables the individual heart to resist public scorn. He may never have realized very precisely the significance of this decision and a thousand others like it, but his fiction from *Huckleberry Finn* on shows his increasing concern with the destiny of the individual in society and his decreasing hope in the ability of the human heart to remain a source of moral vitality.

The problem was a deeply personal one for Clemens, but like so many of his dilemmas and persuasions, it had a high degree of cultural currency. Americans, from the seventeenth century to the present, have been faced with the task of reconciling their ideals of individualism and personal freedom with the fact of power which concentrates in institutions and restricts the individual will. A belief in individualism depends finally on what amounts to religious faith —the assurance that the individual has recourse to a constant source of moral truth. But when this faith weakens, as it has so steadily over the three centuries of American history, then individuals will erect institutions to take its place. The need for predictability, for constancy, for a bulwark against chaos must be satisfied, even at the cost of violating the culture's most sacred precepts.

Clemens wrote *Huckleberry Finn* at a time when Americans still held tenaciously to a belief in the sanctity of the undisciplined will. But it was also a time when such individualism was fostering waste, injustice, and political corruption, and was victimizing a large segment of the population. Before long, Americans would have to reexamine their ideals and learn to live with the institutions they had been forced to create. But in 1885, the relation between the expectations of perfection and the fact of corruption was yet unseen. The prophetic element in *Huckleberry Finn* is its statement that the two are, in fact, irreconcilable.

Like most of Clemens' works, the novel is clearly nostalgic. It recalls a supposed happy time when there was still a place for the unspoiled individual in American life. After realizing that society will not supply the freedom his nature demands, Huck runs off to "the Territory." But in 1885, "the Territory" was largely a fiction, and the statement of the novel remains that individual freedom in its purest sense is no longer possible. So, nostalgic as it is, the book appraises our situation with dark honesty. When literature vizualizes the world of desire, it is not necessarily escaping from reality; it may be depicting the ideals toward which human life continually strives. The Innocent Land, especially in *Huckleberry Finn,* may be taken as the imaginative projection of social ideals, which make the necessary judgment on actuality by contrast. The backward glance may smack of self-indulgence and escape, but it leaves no doubt that the present is unbearable and the future, hopeless. We could, I suppose, argue that the book fails by giving Huck one last chance to run off, by neglecting to reconcile the dream of innocence, symbolized by Huck, with the facts of social existence, symbolized by the life along the river shore. Surely a compromise between the individual and society is possible; we cannot believe that they are mutually exclusive choices. But Clemens felt that they were, and the test of his honesty is that he acknowledged the vulnerability of his fondest ideal, instead of ignoring the contradictions between faith and fact and allowing his dream to dictate a vision of false hope. In his later years, Clemens continued to seek new ''territories,'' in which innocence could fulfill its promise, but he never again suggested that our experience would afford such a theatre of possibility. In a time when visions of doom are still considered unpatriotic, it ill becomes us to demand on theoretical grounds a more courageous moral stand.

6.
The Yankee Pirate

*A CONNECTICUT YANKEE
IN KING ARTHUR'S COURT*

Viewed on the surface only, *A Connecticut Yankee* appears to espouse the values of nineteenth-century American commercial, technological, and social advancement over medieval backwardness and injustice. Yet this surface statement generates an impression of almost unrelieved irony when one analyzes the novel closely. Spirited back to Arthurian England, Hank Morgan turns his Yankee ingenuity loose on the barbaric ignorance of that superstitious and inhumane era. But his attempts to enlighten the Dark Ages by means of inventions and democratic ideals fail miserably. He returns to his own time, having destroyed Arthur's kingdom without putting any viable system in its place. He leaves Camelot a reeking battlefield, poisoned by the putrefying bodies of Arthur's knights, and he knows that the traditions and superstitions of the Old World have thwarted his progressive aims and conquered him. Furthermore, the victory of past over present does not consist simply in its dogged refusal to accept commerce and science but in the seduction of Morgan himself. On his deathbed he pines for his "lost land," his home, and his friends—"all that is dear . . . all that makes life worth the living." [1] Why should a progressive Yankee long for an age that has stubbornly resisted his attempts to improve it? What attractions has backward Camelot for this nineteenth-century advocate of material progress?

Morgan's apparently unaccountable nostalgia contradicts virtu-

84

ally every judgment he has rendered against feudal society throughout the book, and it suggests that those pronouncements have been
incorrect all along. Herein lies the key to the meaning of the novel, I
believe, for as long as we take Morgan's opinions to be Clemens'
personal views the book remains inconclusive and generally unsatisfactory. Only by comparing Morgan's statements with the situations
as they are presented do we come to realize that he represents an
incorrect code of values, that his progressive schemes, not medieval
primitivism, destroy Camelot.

But there can be no doubt that Clemens consciously intended to
demonstrate the wonderful strides mankind had made toward justice
and creature comfort in the centuries since the feudal era. In his
original preface to *A Connecticut Yankee* he says, "My object has
been to group together some of the most odious laws which have had
vogue in the Christian countries within the past eight or ten centuries and illustrate them by the incidents of a story . . . My purpose . . . was to show great and genuine progress in Christendom in
these few later generations toward mercifulness—a wide and general
relaxing of the grip of the law." [2] And in a letter to Howells, written
after the book was completed, he indicates his desire to attack the
institutions which existed in medieval Europe: "Well, my book is
written—let it go. But if it were only to write over again there
wouldn't be so many things left out. They burn in me; and they keep
multiplying and multiplying; but now they can't ever be said. And
besides, they would require a library—and a pen warmed in hell." [3]
This latter statement suggests not only that he intended to criticize
but that somehow his aim had been compromised. Perhaps he realized, however vaguely, that modern America comes off second best to
medieval Europe in the novel, and that this outcome limits the
effectiveness of the criticism.

Clemens' appraisal and Morgan's fate clearly indicate that a sub-
versive influence is at work in the book. Throughout the action some
force keeps Morgan's ideas from assuming credibility and persua-
siveness. This compromising element, I am sure, is Clemens' skepticism
regarding modern progress, which he reveals on several occasions in
A Connecticut Yankee by describing Camelot as an Innocent Land
filled with attractive people, and Hank Morgan as an insensitive

devotee of modern commercial corruption. The conflict between the two is in many ways identical to that which I discussed in the analysis of *Huckleberry Finn:* evil modern society *versus* natural innocence. Hank Morgan invades the Innocent Land of Arthur's England and teaches its happy citizens the way of nineteenth-century America. In so doing he leads them out of innocence and destroys them, realizing too late what he has lost.

This pattern of action appears in Clemens' work as early as *The Innocents Abroad,* in which the traveler initially views Palestine as backward and barbaric, but later succumbs to its atmosphere of tradition and romance. It occurs again in *Roughing It,* when the Greenhorn and his companion invade the sacred wilderness of Tahoe, bent on making a fortune in timber. The natural beauty of the forest seduces them, and their enterprise gives way to a happy acceptance of reposeful, dreamy, inviting nature. Moreover, just as war and commerce have destroyed ancient Palestine, and commercial enterprise ruins the forest at Tahoe, Morgan's commercial and military policies devastate Camelot.

Clemens learned to deliver his criticism of American institutions in the heavily ironic voice of the ''inspired idiot'' when he was working for the Virginia City *Enterprise.* From that time on he employed this persona whenever he wanted to attack injustice and corruption within the system, reserving his own non-ironic voice for praise of progress and the virtues of American democracy. The ''unconsciously'' ironic voice enabled him to express his reservations about the success of the commercial ideal without endangering his reputation as a patriot and a spokesman of his age, upon which he relied for his livelihood. In an address to a gathering of Americans in London, for example, he said, ''This is an age of progress, and ours is a progressive land. A great and glorious land, too—a land which has developed a Washington, a Franklin, a William M. Tweed, a Longfellow, a Motley, a Jay Gould, a Samuel C. Pomeroy, a recent Congress which has never had its equal (in some respects), and a United States Army, which conquered sixty Indians in eight months by tiring them out—which is much better than uncivilized slaughter, God knows.'' [4] By lumping Washington, Franklin, Gould, Tweed, and Pomeroy together he clearly indicates his attitude toward progress without accepting the responsibility for his ''unconscious'' criticism. Again, in a Fulton Day address in 1907 he called the telephone, telegraph, and steamboat ''great American events,'' and then went on to muddle the details of these works and their inventors so that the audience could not possibly take them seriously.[5] His method allowed him to pass his strictures off as pure fun, but he was undoubtedly deeply concerned about the matters in question.

Speaking privately, he was much more direct in his accusations. In his notebook, he wrote, ''Sixty years ago optimist and fool were not synonymous terms. This is a greater change than that wrought by science and invention. It is the mightiest change ever wrought in the world in any sixty years since creation.''[6] And in a letter to Mrs. Fairbanks he said, ''I hate all shades & forms of republican government . . . I always [sic] hated them. . . . With an unrestricted suffrage a country ought to perish because it is founded in wrong & is weak & bad & tyrannical.''[7] These latter comments illustrate Clemens' beliefs in the difference between public and private opinion when they are compared to Hank Morgan's pronouncement: ''Where every man in a state has a vote, brutal laws are impossible.''[8]

Such contradictory attitudes do not denote hypocrisy, by any means. They only evidence the turmoil that went on in Clemens' own mind. Throughout the works that precede *A Connecticut Yankee,* as I trust my previous analyses have shown, similar ambivalent views find expression. At the same time that he was torn between the desire to return to innocence and the urge to make sense out of his adult life, he alternately advocated progress and primitivism. In his public life he seems often to have operated on the assumption that moral and material progress were the lessons of history, the facts of the present, and guides to the future—especially in the United States. Even his private musings, in his more sanguine moods, reflect a measure of this assurance. But in his most personal deliberations, those he conducted on the presentational and symbolic level of his fiction, he betrays a sense of something untrue in such optimism, some hideous, uncontrollable fact of life that prevented beneficent progress and made human history a necessary journey away from goodness, toward evil and despair. His belief in progress established the intended thesis of *A Connecticut Yankee,* while his feelings of doubt—which often underlay his various celebrations of innocence—informed its action.

Since the ultimate meaning of the novel lies in the irony of Morgan's statements, which are often more indicative of his character than of the situations on which he comments, it is possible to arrive at that meaning by analyzing the objective reality which forms the basis for that irony. *A Connecticut Yankee* is formally a frame-story from which the frame narrator disappears when he offers Morgan's manuscript in place of his own account of the action. At that point the novel becomes—like "The Jumping Frog," "Captain Stormfield," and *Huckleberry Finn*—a tale told by a speaker who is unaware that he is reporting only appearances. Only by penetrating the irony of the vernacular speaker's pronouncements can the reader discern the true facts. Three types of evidence disclose the reality behind Morgan's narrative: Clemens' statements of his intention in writing *A Connecticut Yankee;* Morgan's contradictions of Clemens' avowed beliefs, which the author expressed either in previous works or in letters and speeches; and, most important, the employment of the conventions of innocence, which have assumed a specific predictable meaning through continued use in the works of fiction which precede *A Connecticut Yankee.* And this evidence indicates strongly that although Clemens created Morgan as an advocate of progress whose attitudes and actions are to be admired, the hero very soon becomes a seducer of the innocent citizens of Camelot, an evil invader in the Innocent Land.

Clemens conceived Morgan as a representative of the ingenious practicality which he thought America created by its emphasis on individual freedom. Morgan is a natural genius, the product of a political and economic system, not of formal training. Clemens says of him, "This Yankee of mine has neither the refinement nor the weaknesses of a college education; he is a perfect ignoramus; he is the boss of a machine shop; he can build a locomotive or a Colt's revolver, he can put up a telegraph line, but he's an ignoramus, nevertheless." [9] Clemens' insistence on Morgan's ignorance denotes not only his intention to make the Yankee a product of his political environment, it bespeaks also the author's wish to invest his hero with the traits of natural innocence. This impression is further substantiated by Morgan's good-heartedness, which he exhibits when, endangered by a companion's folly, he says, "I had not the heart to tell him his good-hearted foolishness had ruined me and sent me to my death." [10] Then, the frame-narrator notices that Morgan is "barren of sentiment—or poetry in other words"; and he calls him a "curious stranger," an epithet which recalls Christ in *The Innocents Abroad,* Huck Finn in his many disguises, and Philip Traum in *The Mysterious Stranger.* All of these characters are essentially innocent and all receive sympathetic treatment from the author. These traits combined—craftiness, compassion, ignorance (which Clemens reinforces by having Hank speak in the vernacular), practicality, and mystery—link Morgan with Clemens' innocents. *115839*

Inherent within these very characteristics, however, are qualities which make Morgan a destroyer instead of an innocent. Appropriately, these corrupting traits—insensitivity, commercial enterprise, a knack for self-dramatization, and a sense of social respectability— are the same ones which end Tom Sawyer's innocence. Despite his periodic display of compassion, Morgan is so generally callous that he seldom realizes the great boons of the Innocent Land, and the very few perceptions he has never hinder his aims to "improve" Camelot and to glorify himself. He is permanently isolated from nature, the source of Huck's strength, largely because he views it as a means to wealth and self-aggrandizement. He tells a hermit, "You have lived in the woods and lost much by it." [11] His native vernacular is filled with the jargon of modern business, and he delivers his most solemn judgments in these terms. As far as he is concerned, money is the lifeblood of the nation; a piece of good luck is like striking oil, and his main objection to Sandy is that she has no head for business. Like Tom, he is deceitful; he used to put buttons in the collection plate and keep the coins for himself. Also, he devotes his energies to "spreading himself," and he is worried when he is out of the limelight. As he says, "I never care to do a thing in a quiet way, it's got to be theatrical." [12] Finally, he is an inveterate bluenose. He feels that riding alone with Sandy would be improper, he chides the court for its foul speech, he is ashamed to doff his armor in Sandy's presence even though he is fully clothed underneath, and he marries her at last, not because he loves her, but because he thinks she may be "compromised." Although some of these faults may appear slight, they seem to be the ones which prompted Clemens to prophesy that an adult Tom Sawyer would be an "ordinary liar." Even more important, they are the qualities which separate Morgan from the Innocent Land and make him its corruptor rather than its defender.

Morgan's flight back in time begins his adventure, and both the nature of his transportation and his descriptions of his new surroundings signal his entrance into an Innocent Land. Knocked out in a machine shop, he wakes up in "a beautiful broad country landscape." Upon coming to, he is taken prisoner by a knight, who leads him "as one in a dream" to a "faraway town sleeping in a valley by a winding river." Morgan goes on to describe Camelot in more detail: "It was a soft, reposeful summer landscape, as lovely as a dream, and as lonesome as Sunday. The air was full of the smell of flowers, and the buzzing of insects, and the twittering of birds, and there was no stir of life, nothing going on." [13] Like Huck, who falls asleep in his canoe before entering his dream world of innocent nature, Morgan must pass from civilization to rustic Camelot in a deep sleep. The town bears a close resemblance to Tom Sawyer's St. Petersburg, of course, just as the surrounding countryside appears very much like the summer scenes of Cardiff Hill and Jackson's Island.

Even at this early point in the novel Morgan's actions and attitudes presage the role he will play throughout the rest of the novel. Being a man who considers guns, revolvers, and cannon "labor saving machinery," he is permanently alienated from his new idyllic environment. A beautiful little girl, with "peace reflected in her innocent face," renders a prophetic reaction upon seeing him: she is "turned to stone" with horror. Morgan notices that the members of Arthur's court are similarly "childlike and innocent" and that even the knights' battles are like the quarrels of little boys. He elaborates on the characters of these strange people: "There was something very engaging about these great simple hearted creatures, something attractive and loveable. There did not seem to be brains enough in the entire nursery, so to speak, to bait a fish-hook with; but you didn't seem to mind that, after a little, because you soon saw that brains were not needed in a society like that, and indeed would have marred it, hindered it, spoiled its symmetry—perhaps rendered its existence impossible.''[14] His analysis is entirely correct, for he eventually destroys Camelot by exercising his brains to improve it. Unlike Huck, who accepts the repose that the Innocent Land offers, Morgan decides that because he has brains he will ''boss the whole country inside of three months.'' Brains are as destructive in Camelot as they are on Huck's river, but Morgan, filled with the unholy desire to get ahead, plans to employ his wits to remake paradise. As he says, ''I was just another Robinson Crusoe cast away on an uninhabited island, with no society but some more or less tame animals, and if I wanted to make life bearable I must do as he did—invent, contrive, create, reorganize things.''[15] Later he restates his intentions in the clichés of an entrepreneur in the American West (a locale that was the Innocent Land in *Roughing It*) : ''Look at the opportunities here for a man of knowledge, brains, and pluck, and enterprise to sail in and grow up with the country.''

Morgan gets his first opportunity to raise himself to power by using his brains when he recalls that an eclipse of the sun is to occur on the day scheduled for his execution. He is confident that the courtiers will not discover his plan to make some practical magic because, as he says, ''These animals [don't] reason . . . they never put two and two together.''[16] He demonstrates similar assurance about the outcome of his plan when he says, ''I so wanted to gather in that great triumph and be the center of all the nation's wonder and reverence. Besides in a business way it would be the making of me; I knew that.''[17] Again his thinking revolves around a desire for power and monetary gain. When he convinces the king that he can blot out the sun, he exclaims, ''My fortune was made,'' and then demands, ''one per cent of such actual increase of revenue over and above its present amount as [he] may succeed in creating for the state.''[18] After offering this ultimatum, in which he sounds more like a legal contract than a human being, he bemoans the fact that the next eclipse is two years away, concluding, ''If it had been booked for only a month away, I could have sold it short; but, as matters stood, I couldn't seem to cipher out any way to make it do me any good, so I gave up trying.''[19] By this time, then, he is well on his way toward turning his brains into power and wealth, having shown his ability to make nature pay big dividends in fear, glory, and financial gain. At the same time, however, he has laid the foundations of a commercial system that will eventually ruin Arthur's kingdom.

Morgan's next adventure, the destruction of Merlin's tower, pits him against the titular head of medieval superstition. Clemens apparently intended to show modern reason ascending over irrational fear, but the passage is so highly symbolic that a very different meaning emerges. Morgan describes the forces of reason and of traditional belief as they take the field in this contest for the people's allegiance. Of himself he says, ''Here I was, a giant among pygmies, a man among children, a master intelligence among intellectual moles; by all rational measurements the only actually great man in that whole British world.'' [20] And he calls the opposition ''the quaintest and simplest and trustingest race . . . nothing but rabbits.'' Although Morgan's tone is completely contemptuous, his vocabulary gives his statements a meaning different from the one he intends. Remember Clemens' judgments against reason in ''Captain Stormfield'' and *Huckleberry Finn;* and remember, too, that although Morgan scorns the people by calling them animals, Huck says, ''There ain't no harm in a hound nohow,'' and Philip Traum prefers animals to human beings. The basic conflict which runs all through the book is not between reason and superstition, but between the head and the heart, between civilized man and natural man.

Morgan's target in this symbolic battle is not only black magic, but feudal knighthood as well. His description makes the tower the very image of traditional feudalism: ''This old stone tower was very massive—and rather ruinous, too, for it was Roman, and four hundred years old. Yes, and handsome, after a rude fashion, and clothed with ivy from base to summit, as with a shirt of scale mail.'' [21] Yet, when he blows it up he is striking at an institution whose members he has earlier praised: ''There was a fine manliness observable in almost every face; and in some a certain loftiness and sweetness that rebuked your belittling criticisms and stifled them. A most noble benignity and purity reposed in the countenance of him they called Sir Galahad, and likewise in the king's also; and there was majesty and greatness in the giant frame and high bearing of Sir Lancelot of the Lake.'' [22] The reverent tone and attempted stately rhythms of this passage indicate the author's personal attraction for these knights, an affection for tradition which he expressed many times elsewhere. *The Innocents Abroad* is filled with details of venerable antiquity, lovingly set down by the narrator. The hero and heroine of *The American Claimant* solve their problems by returning to England and reassuming the noble title he has previously renounced. *Pudd'n-head Wilson* espouses the values of Southern aristocracy, and makes that tradition second only to the European nobility of the twins. Then, Clemens wrote in the privacy of his notebook, "Essentially, nobilities are foolishness, but if I were a citizen where they prevail I would do my best to get a title, for the consideration it furnishes— that is what we want. In Republics we strive for it with the surest means we have—money." [23] It is not unnatural that the lures of aristocracy and tradition should reassert themselves in *A Connecti-cut Yankee;* especially since Clemens was falling into tremendous financial difficulties at the time he was writing the book. When Morgan destroys the tower, he strikes at a system and an ethic which Clemens periodically admired.

In the early chapters of *A Connecticut Yankee,* Clemens gives the reader only an abstract impression of the values that the Innocent Land represents, by means of landscape descriptions, Morgan's in-consistencies, tone, and vocabulary. But when Morgan meets Sandy, the conflict between civilization and innocence is rendered in terms of a human relationship—the metaphor which Clemens uses to create his most telling effects in *Huckleberry Finn.* Their first encounter establishes the tenor of their future career together, and the attitudes assumed by each persist with only minor variations to the end of the novel. In this initial meeting Morgan is brusque, businesslike, and skeptical. When Sandy introduces herself, he asks for written proof of her identity and allegiance and then calls her "innocent and idiotic" when she cannot understand why he should doubt her word. As she continues to talk, he persistently interrupts with rude, ill-tempered outbursts of exasperation. For the remainder of the book Morgan is patronizing, prudish, and abrupt, while Sandy is con-stantly loyal, loving, and innocent. As a result, the reader's sympa-thies rest predominantly on her side, even though Clemens later has her illustrate aristocratic haughtiness in contrast to Morgan's democratic instincts. Once again a comparison to *Huckleberry Finn* is appropriate, for while Huck learns to revere Jim, Morgan is almost totally separated from Sandy by the innocence he cannot share with her.

When Morgan and Sandy set out in search of adventure, they leave the city and enter the idyllic countryside. Here, as always, Clemens makes the distinction between urban constraint and rustic freedom. The long passage in which Morgan describes the scenery in the first part of the journey is so typical that it is worth transcribing in detail:

> Straight off we were in the country. It was most lovely and pleasant in those sylvan solitudes . . . We saw the ranges of hills, blue with haze, stretching away in billowy perspective to the horizon, with at wide intervals a dim fleck of white or gray on a wave summit. . . . We moved like spirits . . . we dreamed along through glades in the midst of a green light. . . . We left the world behind and entered into the . . . rich gloom of the forest.[24]

Notice the dominant qualities of the setting—haziness, solitude, dreaminess, and somnolent movement—so familiar from other descriptions of the innocent wilderness. The landscape solidifies the impression of innocence which Camelot engenders, and it throws into sharp relief the city, which Morgan is steadily industrializing with his factories.

Morgan is not totally immune to the attractions of this environment. He begins to chafe in his armor and yearns to get out of his clothing. He even reaffirms the symbolic significance of clothes in a comment about institutions: "Institutions are extraneous, they are . . . mere clothing, and clothing can wear out, become ragged, cease to be comfortable, cease to protect the body from winter, disease, and death." [25] The gauds and finery which he covets in society become cumbersome and expendable in nature. Even the social status which they represent seems to fall away, and Morgan says, very uncharacteristically, "I am not better than others." Unfortunately, he cannot maintain his dreamy egalitarian emotions in the society which he erects in Camelot. As he regains his desire to array himself, he also reiterates his conviction that he is better than anyone else in Arthur's kingdom. When the people treat him as "some kind of superior being,'' he says, ''And I was.'' He holds to this view, moreover, even though he sees the callousness of rank and the humility of servitude as ''the result of the same cause in both cases: the possessor's inbred custom of regarding himself as a superior being.''

All of these contradictions appear to be the result of the conflict between Clemens' intentions and his beliefs. Although Morgan is supposed to be the worthy champion of democracy, industrialization, and reason, he arraigns himself before the bar of innocence and tradition every time he acts in this capacity. On the other hand, when he succumbs momentarily to the lures of nature, he belies his position as an advocate of commercial progress. These inconsistencies should become more evident and more enlightening in terms of their final artistic solution as I examine Morgan's diagnosis of English problems and his attempts to rectify them.

In the first place, Morgan sees that the natives of Camelot have no brains, that they have no head for business, that they do not reason. Second, he sees that they are enslaved by an inbred adherence to tradition. The Church and the aristocracy keep the people in perpetual servitude. For these two reasons, he deduces, they have made no progress; they have no commercial system, no telephones, no rapid transportation, no scientific inventions of any kind. But because he has brains and can reason he considers himself a superior creature, and as such he expects to be a figure of public adoration. In place of the superstitious magic of the Church, he wants to install the ''magic of science.'' For the nobility he will substitute a moneyed aristocracy who claim their position by their financial holdings. To make this last change possible he must industrialize the nation and fill its homes with the mechanical appurtenances of civilization. In place of the whole ancient civilization he wants to establish a mercantile economy. Clearly he is bent on replacing old institutions with new ones. But Clemens' deepest sympathies lay not with institutions but with innocence; and he was particularly suspicious of business, which disenchanted him and caused him so much anxiety during his later years.

Morgan begins his program of civilization by building factories— those slave-pens which Clemens attacks, anachronistically, in *The Mysterious Stranger*. His next step is to establish a free press, which turns out to be merely irresponsible. Morgan, however, approves of the "whoop and crash and lurid description" of newspaper writing and is only disturbed by his reporter's lack of skill in this vein. He institutes advertising as an "uplifting" and civilizing influence, and proceeds to paint the rocks with his slogans. (Significantly, the ethics of knight-errantry are not inherently ridiculous, and the knights appear absurd only when they begin to carry sandwich-boards.) Morgan's proudest achievement is his telephone. While he may have been momentarily seduced by Sandy and the dreamy torpor of the Innocent Land, the advent of this instrument reminds him "what a creepy, dull, inanimate horror this land had been to [him] all these years," and how he had been in "such a stifled condition of mind as to have grown used to it almost beyond the power to notice it." In the same episode, however, he exclaims that the telephone has made a "Valley of Hellishness" out of the "Valley of Holiness."

Another of his great accomplishments is his educational program. Fulfilling his role as the seducer, he goes to work on the youth of England, training them for factory jobs, instructing them in scientific technology. He refuses to bother with those whom tradition has already corrupted; anyone ignorant of "scientific war," he says, is useless. As part of this program he sends the knights out as "missionaries" of civilization. This term is especially meaningful when examined in the light of Clemens' views on missionaries, which he sums up so thoroughly in "To a Person Sitting in Darkness." Like the nineteenth-century variety that Clemens hated, Morgan's evangelists kill those customers who do not choose to accept their wares. These are the boons which Morgan brings to "the good children" of Camelot—that "curious country . . . for men and women that never get old." By these means he turns England into "the only nation on earth standing ready to blossom into civilization."

During his first introduction to Arthurian society, his rise to power, and his quest for adventure, Morgan speaks alternately in the vernacular and in a relatively educated idiom. This alternation of speaking styles results from the same contradiction of intention and belief that pervades the episodes already examined and can provide a method of understanding similar problems to follow. In *Huckleberry Finn*, especially, the vernacular voice asserts a code of ethics completely antithetical to civilized society and its constraining institu-

tions of money, slavery, government, and organized religion. In that
earlier book, too, the vernacular voice shares the weaknesses of innocence itself. Because of its limited power to generalize and to abstract ideas from experience, it maintains itself by avoiding contact
with the intellectual problems of civilization. Just as innocence survives through flight from evil, the vernacular survives by avoiding
sustained rational discourse. While the vernacular voice was appropriate to Huck, whom Clemens conceived as an innocent who endures
by evading evil, it ill becomes Morgan, who means to analyze England's social problems and to erect progressive institutions to solve
them. Whenever Morgan rationalizes his position in Camelot, decides
to take advantage of his brains, and sets out to improve the social
system, then, he speaks in long polemical passages whose style is
distinctly non-vernacular. On his trip with Sandy, for example, he
comes across a group of peasants mending a road and explains their
status in these words:

> They were not slaves. . . . By a sarcasm of the law they were freemen.
> Seven-tenths of the free population of the country were of just
> their class and degree . . . which is to say they were . . . the actual
> Nation; . . . to subtract them would have been to subtract the Nation
> and leave behind some dregs . . . in the shape of a king, nobility
> and gentry. . . . And yet, by ingenious contrivance, this gilded
> minority, instead of being in the tail of the procession where it
> belonged, was marching head up and banners flying at the other end
> of it; had elected itself to be the Nation.[26]

He goes on to discuss the role of the Church in this inverted social
order, continually expressing his disgust for the system.

When Sandy and Morgan meet the workers, it is instructive to
notice, Sandy behaves like an aristocrat, refusing to associate with
these lowly ''freemen,'' while Morgan sees their true political value
and sides with them against the aristocratic minority. Such episodes,
it is plain, embody the original intention of the book: to chastise
backward political measures from a nineteenth-century, democratic
point of view. But Morgan's polemical speeches appear mainly as
interruptions in the novel. Whenever he begins to discuss medieval
society at length, the action ceases, and the reader is treated to
several pages of sustained theoretical analysis. On the other hand,

when the action resumes, the whole structure of ideas which Morgan has so carefully articulated steadily disintegrates. As he regains his vernacular voice, the people of Camelot become once again representatives of a happy, innocent, traditional way of life, instead of participants in an unjust political system. But because Morgan continues his program of improvement, his vernacular speeches serve only to comment ironically on his own beliefs; they almost never ally him with the powers of innocence. Clemens' progressive aims, in short, could not be stated in the vernacular nor in terms of the action, both of which continually subvert his intentions. His beliefs, however, find expression in Morgan's ignorant speech, which ironically criticizes progress, and in the action, which shows progress destroying an Innocent Land.

The distinction between Morgan as a vernacular speaker and Morgan as an advocate of Clemens' intended thesis is nowhere more evident, perhaps, than in his tour of England with the disguised king. During this sojourn Morgan assumes a new pose. Instead of being an outsider who is introduced into a strange land, he becomes Arthur's guide through the lower depths of medieval society. He is at home in this world, being a champion of the people and their right to govern themselves, and as such he can effectively instruct the king in the evils of political oppression. This function differs substantially from the one he fulfills elsewhere in the book, and it corresponds generally to the personality he exhibits in the non-vernacular passages just discussed. The initiation of the king seems to translate most satisfactorily the intended thesis into action. However, it remains a single instance of successfully applied progress surrounded by chapters which belie such progress. Furthermore, these ten chapters, in which Morgan teaches Arthur the injustice of his laws, concentrate almost solely on political measures and ignore the saving graces of science and commerce. Democracy and the enfranchisement of the individual seem to have been closer to Clemens' heart than commerce and technology, for democracy is a political ethic very much in tune with innocence: both rely on natural goodness and wisdom. Whatever Clemens may have really thought about the ability of citizens to govern themselves, he apparently wanted to believe that man possessed the gifts which make democracy possible. Consequently, as long as he concentrated on the ideals of self-government and avoided the dubious virtues of material progress, as in the chapters under discussion here, he could make Morgan the admirable spokesman of ideas in which he himself concurred.

In this episode Morgan resembles Miles Hendon of *The Prince and the Pauper,* who guides Edward through his kingdom and teaches him the folly of regal severity. Like Miles, Morgan prevents the king from acting like a nobleman and thereby saves him from numerous difficulties. Like Miles, too, he takes the king's punishments and receives his humble gratitude for these noble acts. The most significant resemblance between Miles and the Yankee, however, is that both relate the objective reality behind each adventure, enabling the reader to perceive the folly of the king's attitude. In connection with this function, both comment on the monarch's progress toward humility and wisdom, detailing the effects of experience on their respective wards. Plainly, Morgan deserves the reader's sympathy in these chapters; as the reporter of reality he relinquishes his ironic voice, which has subverted his position so far, and he achieves a stature not available to him anywhere else in the novel.

As Morgan assumes his new role, the moral cosmos surrounding the action changes accordingly. So far, Morgan has represented progressive social institutions in an Innocent Land; now he supports natural man in his struggle against evil society. Contrary to the democratic principles which inform the action, however, the masses often come in for their share of the criticism, especially when they form into mobs. The democratic ideal holds only as long as it represents natural innocence; when it runs counter to this ideal the action loses its political significance and upholds the isolated good man— though he be a king—over the peasant. Democracy is important only insofar as it embraces the idea of natural goodness; it ceases to support the action when it must enforce the will of the social majority over the solitary individual. Morgan, then, takes a stand—like Huck's although more articulate—against institutions which threaten individual freedom. Adhering to the more anarchical elements of the democratic ideal which ostensibly underlies this episode, Morgan sides momentarily with innocence—the state which he persistently undermines elsewhere in the novel.

At the beginning of their journey Morgan succinctly outlines his relationship to the king: "If you have ever seen an active, heedless, enterprising child going diligently out of one mischief and into another all day long, and an anxious mother at its heels all the while, and just saving it from drowning itself or breaking its neck with each new experiment, you've seen the king and me." [27] By calling him a child and by referring to his training as a "novitiate," Morgan points up the educational aspect of the adventure. He then explains the purpose of this education by commenting on the king's character: "He was born [prejudiced], educated so, his veins were full of ancestral blood that was rotten with this sort of unconscious brutality, brought down by inheritance from a long procession of hearts that had each done its share toward poisoning the stream." [28] The king, in other words, has a faulty conscience; and Morgan's aim is to remove his aristocratic prejudices by acquainting him with the effects of such ideas.

Given this situation, one should expect the king to grow increasingly benevolent and charitable, as in fact he does. But one should also expect this new awareness to depend on experiences which demonstrate the goodness of the people and the evil of the rulers. But, as I explained earlier, democracy guides the action only insofar as it attests to man's essential innocence; as a principle of group action it fails to apply. Consequently, when Clemens presents Arthur as the symbol of hereditary nobility and political oppression, "he is just a cheap and hollow artificiality," but when he makes Arthur the representative of natural goodness, the king behaves nobly and admirably. For example, if the democratic idea held true throughout this episode, the peasants would invariably represent virtue and the king, vice. But when Arthur attends the woman stricken with smallpox, whom the mob has deserted, he stops being an evil king and becomes a good man.

Morgan outlines this thesis—that man is basically good and becomes evil only through association with institutions—several times during the journey. Looking ahead to his own time, he remarks that the baseness of the "poor whites" is due entirely to the institution of slavery in their midst. Later, when the king shows that he can understand aristocratic brutality, Morgan exclaims, "A man *is* a

100

man at bottom. Whole ages of abuse and oppression cannot crush the manhood out of him.'' [29] That is, although aristocratic institutions have degraded Arthur's natural innocence, that quality remains latent in his nature and requires only freedom to act. Man can return to his innocent state by casting off his institutionalized ideas as if they were garments. Again, after his own attempts to make the king act like a serf have failed and after the slave-driver has not been able to subdue Arthur's pride and bearing, Morgan says, ''The fact is, the king was a good deal more than a king, he was a man; and when a man is a man, you can't knock it out of him.'' [30]

The king completes his education on the scaffold, awaiting death. Fully apprised of the horrors which his laws have made possible, he possesses a new charity and humility—or rather, an old compassion reborn through freedom and experience. Curiously, however, Morgan describes Arthur's triumph in words which deny the democratic beliefs he upheld at the outset of the journey. He says, ''And as he stood apart there, receiving his homage in rags, I thought to myself, well really there *is* something peculiarly grand about the gait of a king after all.'' [31] Morgan has arrived at this state of mind via a paralogistic path, which began with his hatred of kingship and ends with his glorification of it. In the beginning he supported democracy and the rights of the citizenry. His role as a spokesman for the nineteenth-century American way permitted him to take such a stand. Very soon, however, Clemens' feelings for innocence cause Morgan to support individual nobility against mob constraint and to aver man's basic goodness. Then in the process of investing his sympathies in the king, who defies social convention and the cowardly mob as he learns his lessons, Morgan transfers these sympathies from Arthur as an individual to Arthur as a king. These are signs of this growing allegiance to kingship throughout these chapters, but they are normally overshadowed by the emphasis on democracy and innocence. For example, Morgan mentions several times that the king has too much style to look like a peasant. Then, commenting on Arthur's intelligence, he says, ''It was a wise head. A peasant's cap was no safe disguise for it; you could know it for a king's under a diving-bell, if you could hear it work its intellect.'' [32] Similarly, the king's inbred chivalry prompts many of his brave acts and shows forth whenever he is confronted by danger and harassment. In short, Morgan translates natural nobility into political nobility, and he concludes by openly asserting the values which make themselves known elsewhere in the book through the action and through the Yankee's vernacular, ironic statements.

The next chapter, which recounts Morgan's fight with the knights, returns to the method and tone of those chapters which precede the king's initiation. Once again Morgan is the opportunist, the advocate of science and progress. There is virtually no indication here of his recent defection from nineteenth-century ethics. The events of the preceding ten chapters are left hanging in space. Morgan now sets out to destroy the knights who saved him from the scaffold, to erase the traditions which made Arthur brave and noble during his experiences as a slave. Summing up the symbolic value of the forthcoming combat, he says, ''So the world thought there was a vast matter at stake here, and the world was right, but it was not the one they had in their minds. No, a far vaster one was upon the cast of this die; *the life of knight-errantry.* I was a champion, it was true, but not of the frivolous black arts, I was the champion of hard unsentimental common sense and reason. I was entering the lists to either destroy knight-errantry or be its victim.''[33] So, he intends to defeat the men whose virtue he has previously associated with innocence and tradition—the only values which have sustained themselves in action so far in the novel.

The fight itself is brief and decisive; knight-errantry goes down to defeat before Morgan's pistol. Very little credit can possibly accrue to the Yankee in this encounter, however, for, being armed with a gun, he is in no real danger. Sir Sagramor discredits the knights' heroism when he tries to kill Morgan, whom he believes to be unarmed. Still, the rest of the knights eagerly answer Morgan's challenge, although they know that Sagramor has been killed by magic. This triumph is Morgan's biggest step up to supreme power, and he constructs it out of dead bodies. From this point on, his victories are all based on destruction and death.

Having subdued feudalism, the nobility, and knight-errantry, Morgan now brings his clandestine operations into the open. In three years' time he has turned England into a nineteenth-century America. His description of this "modern paradise" is instructive, for it lists warships along with colleges, concentrates on the more ludicrous aspects of a growing industrial civilization, and mentions the beginnings of official corruption. He puts the aristocracy to work as railway conductors, death-dealing "missionaries" of civilization, and baseball players. And most important of all, he turns the Round Table into a stock exchange, thereby erecting the institution which precipitates the final catastrophe.

When the interdict strikes, Morgan is on the Continent. Upon returning he learns from Clarence that Lancelot's manipulations of the stock market have caused disaster. (The knight may well have learned his tricks from Morgan, who sold his stock in the performing pilgrim to the knights when the bottom began to drop out of the market.) Angered at having been swindled by Lancelot, several knights have informed Arthur of Guenever's infidelity. England has divided itself into two warring camps, the king and the best of the knights are dead, and to stop the slaughter the Church has snuffed out Morgan's "beautiful civilization." Clarence warns the Yankee that he must prepare for war; the Church recognizes him as a threat to its supremacy and is sending the army against him.

Morgan makes his final stand in Merlin's cave, where he and his fifty-two loyal boys prepare to meet the enemy. Morgan has trained these youths in the arts of scientific war, and after conquering their reluctance to kill their own people, he leads them in a devastating battle with the knights. During this encounter Morgan becomes a rabble-rouser, urging his followers on with cliché-ridden messages of exhortation. There is no question of individualism and innocence here; his army behaves exactly like the mobs who excite so much scorn during the tour with Arthur. In the end the fifty-four insurgents are "masters of England." Morgan concludes several pages of lurid description of the war with the terse comment, "Twenty-five thousand men lay dead around us."

The victory is an empty one, however. The bodies of the knights form an insurmountable wall, and as they putrefy they poison the victors one by one. Clarence sums up the irony of the situation when he says, "We had conquered; in turn we were conquered"; and Merlin reiterates the paradox as if it were a curse. Morgan falls into a deep sleep and thus returns to the nineteenth century. Ranting deliriously, he confuses his dreams with reality and longs for his lost land, his wife and his child. The Innocent Land conquers finally, not by killing him, but by making him yearn for the happy life he has destroyed with war and commerce.

In *A Connecticut Yankee,* to recapitulate, Clemens intends to show Morgan as a champion of nineteenth-century America with its institutions of democracy, commerce, industry, science, and unlimited progress. To provide an appropriate setting for the Yankee's adventures he creates a medieval England strangled by an hereditary aristocracy, an established church, and inhuman laws. Through the story which results from this comparison of the dark past and the enlightened present, Clemens purports to show the great progress mankind has made since the sixth century—a progress in which he officially believed. However, his gnawing distrust of commercialism and social institutions, and his continued interest in the innocent past, with its agrarian economy and its stable traditions, subverted these aims. These forces caused him to make Morgan an unscrupulous opportunist, bent on replacing old institutions with new ones merely for the sake of self-glorification and personal gain. Camelot appears in the novel, not always as a backward and inhuman historical era, but often as the dreamy, idyllic land of innocence. As Morgan attempts to improve this land by effecting civilized reforms, he destroys it, realizing too late his terrible loss.

Clemens tells his story in a tone of sustained but largely unintentional irony. In doing so he betrays once again his convictions that man is basically good and that evil institutions have smothered his innocence. As in *Huckleberry Finn,* he shows how vulnerable innocence is to external evil, how easily it can be destroyed by society and its institutions. Perhaps the most telling irony of all appears in a statement by Morgan which clearly suggests Clemens' opinion of modern America: ''What would I amount to in the twentieth century? I should be a foreman of a factory, that is about all; and you could drag a seine down-street any day and catch a hundred better than myself.'' [34]

7.

The Saint

JOAN OF ARC

WHATEVER ITS LITERARY faults—and there are many —*Joan of Arc* assumes a position of considerable importance in any discussion of Clemens' fiction, for it contains some of his most explicit statements about the nature and fate of innocence. I have argued in previous chapters that the concept of innocence appears in the early books largely in the narrative techniques and methods of characterization which Clemens inherited from various literary and sub-literary sources; that it receives more direct attention in *The Gilded Age,* although it remains incidental to the main purpose of that novel; that while it retains its secondary status in *The Prince and the Pauper,* "Old Times on the Mississippi," and *Tom Sawyer,* its various fictional properties harden into conventions in these works; that it poses the pre-eminent problem in *Huckleberry Finn;* and that its attractions for Clemens subvert the intentions of *A Connecticut Yankee.* This development clearly shows Clemens' rising interest in the meaning of good and evil, as well as his growing tendency to simplify those ideas by repeatedly representing them in terms of a basic conflict: innocent natural man against corrupt institutionalized society.

Within this larger development—the growing thematic importance of innocence—there is, as I have also attempted to demonstrate, Clemens' increasing belief in the vulnerability of innocence. In *Roughing It* and "Captain Stormfield" innocence prospers and fulfills itself in a fanciful land of freedom and possibility. In *The*

Gilded Age Laura makes a brief, abortive attempt to utilize her new knowledge of evil, but succumbs, finally, to despair and disenchantment. In ''Old Times on the Mississippi'' the Cub's story simply stops when he learns to perceive the ugliness and evil of reality. Tom Canty suggests that innocence can right social wrongs; but his power comes largely from the institution of monarchy, not from innocence itself. Society seduces Tom Sawyer and makes him a wealthy, respectable, ''ordinary liar.'' Huck retains his innocence only by carefully avoiding any compromise with civilization; and Morgan, the champion of modern institutions, corrupts and destroys Camelot as he leads its happy citizens out of innocence. The logical conclusion to be drawn from this development is that innocence is an ideal which cannot survive when confronted by reality. It endures only in the dream state, in the idyllic, pastoral, mysterious setting of the Delectable Land.

Clemens objectifies this logical conclusion by presenting Joan of Arc as an inviolable symbol of innocence, rather than as a human being who is subject to the wiles and malice of institutionalized society.[1] Basing his story on apocryphal contemporary accounts of her trial, he depicts her as a superhuman embodiment of the ideal, retaining her innocence by means of a mystical power. The less enduring purity of the mortals in the book—Le Sieur de Conte, Noel, and the rest of Joan's companions—turns to disenchantment and bitterness, but she remains uncorrupted by virtue of her divine nature. Innocence has the ability to influence action once again; but in this case that influence is entirely mystical, not naturalistic. Unlike Tom Canty, who delivers beneficial pronouncements from his throne, Joan exudes a radiant warmth which mysteriously strengthens her followers. Huck retains his innocence by running from evil; Joan keeps hers because she is above the worldly forces which attempt to seduce her.

Clemens' attitude toward innocence in *Joan of Arc* is revealed mainly in the narrative technique and in the language used to describe Joan. Le Sieur de Conte, Joan's childhood companion, tells her story, using a set of images drawn from the conventions which I have described in earlier chapters. As he recounts the events of her remarkable career, his own attitude undergoes a transformation from innocent optimism to disillusionment and nostalgia. In other words, the novel deals with the narrator's initiation, while Joan remains a symbol of the innocence he loses through his experience with evil. *Joan of Arc* presents innocence as a spiritual ideal, a state of mind which cannot exist in the corrupt and hostile world of reality.

Le Sieur Louis de Conte narrates the events of the book from a point outside the action. His opening remarks define the point of view: "This is the year 1492. I am eighty-two years of age. The things which I am going to tell you are things which I saw myself as a child and as a youth." [2] The narrative voice, like that of *Roughing It*, belongs to an older man who will describe a series of experiences as he saw them through youthful eyes. As in the Western travel-book, this technique gives the text depth in time, enabling Le Sieur to contrast his youthful and adult opinions. Consequently, while the novel relates his progress from romantic hopefulness to disenchanted pessimism, virtually every statement contains these two disparate attitudes. Throughout the story the reader is aware of the vast difference between youth and age, happiness and despair. Furthermore, this contrast is doubly important because Le Sieur becomes disillusioned as a result of witnessing Joan's fate. The narrative mode, then, depicts the change that comes over man as earthly innocence is destroyed.

In the beginning de Conte is a happy, heedless child in Domremy, a village lying on a river near a flowery plain and a great forest. With Joan and the rest of his companions he plays about the Fairy Tree, believing in its mysteries and singing its hymn of perpetual youth. This arcadian setting is already familiar, but Clemens has injected an element of the supernatural here with the children's fairy playmates. Innocence is more explicitly spiritual than in any of the previous works.

The village church is characteristically hostile to innocence, however, and the priest exorcizes the tree, banishing its spirits. The narrator foreshadows events to come as he describes the effects of the exorcism: "The great tree . . . was never afterward quite as much to us as it had been before, but it was always dear; is dear to me yet when I go there, now, once a year in my old age, to sit under it and bring back the lost playmates of my youth and group them about me and look upon their faces through my tears and break my heart, oh, my God!''[3] Shamelessly sentimental as this passage is, it describes the twin fates of innocence and Joan. The tree is the children's symbol of youth and freedom, and when the Church destroys it, much of its charm is lost. Like the tree, Joan dies at the hands of the Church, and although her power diminishes at her death, she too remains in Le Sieur's memory. The narrative mode enables de Conte to foreshadow the action by contrasting his present despair and past happiness as well as by giving the history of the tree a portentous significance.

Le Sieur's development begins as he discovers the world outside Domremy. After learning about the disastrous Treaty of Troyes, he and his friends show their romantic vision of war as they plan strategies to free France from the English. But he does not have an opportunity to do more than dream until Joan has her vision and sets out to gather aid for her mission. During the early days of the campaign, before there has been any actual combat, he remains a romantic, optimistic dreamer, falling in love, writing sentimental poetry, showing off for his girl friend. The siege of Orleans introduces him to battle, and his reactions to the grim reality resemble those of the recruit in ''A Campaign that Failed.'' Still, the siege ends in a great victory, and Joan is on the rise; so his enthusiasm, although tempered, is for the most part undiminished.

Before the battle of Jargeau, de Conte and his friends are confident and hopeful about its outcome. He describes the scene in words which keep before the reader's eyes the young and the old Le Sieur: ''After supper some lively young folk whom we knew came in, and we presently forgot that we were soldiers, and only remembered that we were boys and girls and full of animal spirits and long-pent fun; and so there was dancing and games, and romps, and screams of laughter—just as extravagant and innocent and noisy a good time as ever I had in my life. Dear, dear, how long ago it was!—and I was young then.''[4] The narrator seldom relates a situation like this without contrasting with it his retrospective impressions. In this way he repeatedly asserts the fleeting aspect of youthful innocence and foreshadows the disasters to follow.

The first real break in Le Sieur's optimism comes with the realization that Joan has seen the vision of the Fairy Tree, which means that she will die shortly. His reaction is mostly a preparation for more devastating experiences to come, however, for he cannot really believe that Joan can die. As he says in his usual reminiscent manner, "She was to die; and so soon. I had never dreamed of that. How could I, and she so strong and fresh and young, and every day earning a new right to a peaceful and honored old age? For at that time I thought old age valuable. I do not know why, but I thought so. All young people think it, I believe, they being ignorant and full of superstitions." [5] Passages like this one not only show Le Sieur's movement toward disenchantment, they also emphasize the connection between his attitudes and Joan's history. His comments upon this occasion typify those he makes about Joan all through the book: one can usually substitute "innocence" for Joan's name and not impair the sense. I shall comment upon this matter in detail when I examine the imagery which fills the descriptions of her, but I cannot overemphasize how closely Joan relates to Le Sieur's innocence.

The acts of treachery which Joan suffers throughout her imprisonment and trial further undermine Le Sieur's optimism and happiness. At first he believes that France will ransom Joan from the English, who have captured her; but in retrospect he muses, "I believed [it], for I was young and had not yet found out the littleness and meanness of our poor human race, which brags about itself so much, and thinks it is better and higher than the other animals." [6] He is not far from knowing the baseness of men at this point, however. The events which follow steadily reduce his remaining hopes of happiness. First he learns that Joan has been sold to the English, and this piece of news has a peculiar effect on him and Noel: the stream of their laughter is "dried at its source." As I shall show later, Joan's laughter has magic powers, and one main trait which sets children apart from adults in the book is their ability to laugh. Noel then speaks Le Sieur's own thoughts when he comments on another companion's early death: "He drained the cup of glory to the last drop, and went jubilant to his peace, blessedly spared all part in the disaster which was to follow. What luck, what luck! And we? What was our sin that we are still here; we who have also earned our place with the happy dead?"[7] The death-wish, as in the case of Laura, follows hard upon the loss of hope and the childish illusions of innocence.

All that is left to Le Sieur after the trial, save a supreme admiration for Joan's indomitable spirit, are the last remnants of his optimism. Even on the day of her execution he believes that the French will save her. He imagines that the monks who have come to witness the burning are patriots in disguise. Again the older narrator attributes such hope to youth, saying, "We were young then; yes, we were young," and suggesting that optimism is a folly peculiar to ignorant children. Finally, he realizes that he is destined to live out his life with nothing but bitter memories to fill his thoughts, and he indulges in some more sentimental ramblings as Joan dies at the stake. The inevitable nostalgia follows, years later, as he surveys the faces of old acquaintances at Joan's rehabilitation trials; his story closes with a final paean to Joan, "a slender girl in her first young bloom, with the martyr's crown upon her head."

The obvious sentimentality of Le Sieur's story needs no further comment, but two points in connection with his development need emphasis. First, his own history is that of the happy innocent who leaves his idyllic boyhood home to encounter the shocks of the real world and to be beaten down by them. His fate offers absolutely no mitigation; man is destined to despair because reality is treacherous and malignant. Only innocence makes life bearable, and it does not last. Eventually the arresting forces of society invade its pastoral world and destroy it. After that only a few happy memories remain, and these only make the present more bitter. The second point is that Le Sieur's happiness and optimism hang on Joan's fate. While she prospers and inspires action, her followers maintain their zeal, but as she succumbs to the external evils which finally destroy her, Le Sieur grows weary and desperate. The connection between his innocence and her experiences, furthermore, is by no means coincidental.

Joan's symbolic significance appears most explicitly in the description of her march to the stake. She leaves her cell and walks, bathed in sunlight, through crowds of peasants, who kneel with lighted candles as she passes by. Le Sieur continues,

110

And so it was all the way: thousands upon thousands massed upon their knees and stretching far down the distances, thick-sown with faint yellow candle-flames, like a field starred with golden flowers.

But there were some that did not kneel; these were the English soldiers. They stood elbow to elbow, on each side of Joan's road, and walled it in, all the way; and behind these living walls knelt the multitudes.[8]

Joan is the sun, giving life to the people. They are flowers and depend on her for nourishment; but the soldiers, who represent the institutions of church and state, separate her from her devoted followers, leaving them in the shadows to die for want of sustenance. This image is repeated with variations and extensions throughout the novel, making her an innocent, a life-giving force, a child of nature, an enemy to institutions, a superhuman creature, and a patriot.

The sum of Joan's characteristics—freedom, closeness to nature, youth, compassion—show her to be an innocent, and Clemens comments explicitly on her virtues in his essay "St. Joan of Arc," written originally as an introduction to the novel. In one passage he says,

She was gentle and winning and affectionate; she loved her home and her friends and her village life; she was miserable in the presence of pain and suffering; she was full of compassion; . . . she was forgiving, generous, unselfish, magnanimous; she was pure from spot or stain of baseness.[9]

Besides reviewing the properties peculiar to innocence, this list emphasizes Joan's contact with nature and the sinlessness of natural man. Le Sieur, as I shall show, invariably states Joan's affection for her home in terms of her longing for the woods and fields outside her village, especially for the Fairy Tree. Further, the words "spot or stain" suggest that sin is applied from without, that man is born free of baseness and acquires it in life. Although both the language and the concept are commonplace, they support the idea that Clemens considered man to be innocent by nature. Clemens reiterates this suggestion of external evil when he discusses Joan's "unbought grace of youth." Innocence is natural and peculiar to childhood, and Joan is the very image of innocence.

111

The mystical quality of Joan's innocence awes those who see her, and its effulgence generates life and strength in her followers. As she enters the palace for her first interview with the king, her presence stuns the courtiers. Le Sieur says, "The eyes of all were fixed upon Joan in a gaze of wonder which was half worship, and which seemed to say, 'How sweet—how lovely—how divine!' . . . they had the look of people who are under the enchantment of a vision." [10] Joan's historical career lends support to Clemens' interpretation, also, and the narrator calls her mission "the rescue and regeneration of the kingdom." I mentioned earlier that laughter signifies innocence; Joan's laughter, appropriately, makes "old people feel young again." Most of her revivifying power goes to her soldiers, who value her "as the fruitful earth values the sun." She makes them fight on when they are certain that they are beaten, for she has the ability to "blow the breath of life and valor into dead corpses"; and Clemens remarks in his essay, "She was the only heart [her men] had." [11] Le Sieur reviews her effect on her country, repeating the dominant sun imagery:

> She was the sun that melted the frozen torrents and set them boiling; with that sun removed, they froze again, and the army and all France became what they had been before, mere dead corpses—that and nothing more; incapable of thought, hope, ambition, or emotion. [12]

When her captors finally burn her at the stake, the narrator interprets her death as a loss to the whole world: "Yes, she was gone from us: JOAN OF ARC! What little words they are to tell of a rich world made empty and poor!" [13] By depicting the innocent's power as miraculous, then, Clemens enables Joan to surmount the difficulties which generally prevent his innocents from acting. As a human trait, innocence is powerless; but raised to the level of a divine force, it can override evil and effect beneficial results.

Joan derives her marvelous power almost entirely from nature, and she remains throughout the novel a heroine of nature in combat with civilized artificiality. To make Joan represent natural rightness, Clemens transforms the elements of Christian mysticism contained in her history, fitting them into the largely pantheistic scheme which underlies his whole conception of innocence. Joan is the chosen leader of her companions because she is the closest to nature. Le

Sieur calls her the "born child of the sun and of all happy free creatures," and he explains in detail her love for animals and her hatred for cages and fetters. With her native eloquence she defends the Fairy Tree against the village priest, thereby allying herself with nature against organized religion. Furthermore, St. Michael appears to her under the tree, not in church; and as he approaches, "all the birds burst forth in song . . . in an act of worship."

Because she receives her strength from the pastoral environment of Domremy, she is reluctant to leave home for the outside world; when she does set out, her thoughts remain always with her happy life near the Tree. Le Sieur continually refers to her career in the wars and to her imprisonment as an exile, recalling the words of the children's song:

> And when in exile wand'ring we
> Shall fainting yearn for glimpse of thee,
> O rise upon our sight! [14]

Furthermore, according to the legend of Domremy, a vision of the Tree signals approaching death; and Le Sieur considers death, the return to God, and the return to the Tree identical, since all mean release from exile in the world. When he notices Joan's willingness to die, for example, he says, "The death-warning had nothing dismal about it for her; no, it was remission from exile, it was leave to come home." [15]

Joan's native home—particularly the outlying meadows and woods—denotes freedom and closeness to divine nature, while the palaces, prisons, and courts which she inhabits as an exile symbolize mortal constraint. Le Sieur very often characterizes her sufferings in images which reflect Joan's own feeling about confined animals. He calls her a "caged eagle" many times and he says on one occasion, "She was an out-of-doors creature by nature and habit, but now she was shut up day and night like a caged animal." [16] To underscore the impression of a "free spirit" in chains, he precedes a description of her dark cell with a long paragraph on the natural beauties of spring flourishing outside her prison.

As the symbol of free nature, Joan takes her stand from the beginning against institutions. She represents native genius, combatting the malignant intellectualism of the courts. Awed by her skill in evading the legal wiles of her inquisitors, Le Sieur remarks, "I think these vast powers and capacities were born in her, and that she applied them by an intuition which could not err." [17] Elsewhere he attributes this same sagacity to "the protecting luck which attends upon ignorance and innocence." Describing the members of the court, he betrays Clemens' anti-intellectual attitude, calling the judges "Fifty distinguished ecclesiastics, men of high degree in the Church, of clear-cut intellectual faces, men of deep learning, veteran adepts in casuistry, practiced setters of traps for ignorant minds and unwary feet." [18] Notice the tone here: "ignorant" has no bad connotations, since he uses it as a synonym for "innocence"; intellectuals are those who seduce the innocent with their artificial, casuistic learning, the science of the institutions. In another description of Joan's examiners, Le Sieur links Joan to Huck as he highlights the difference between natural wisdom and civilized knowledge: "She faced that great company of erudite doctors of law and theology, and by the help of no art learned in the schools, but using only the enchantments that were hers by nature of youth, sincerity, a voice soft and musical, and an eloquence whose source was the heart, not the head, she laid that spell upon them." [19] This passage also explains why Joan can retain her innocence in a constraining environment while Huck's finer instincts are smothered in society: Joan's innocence is "enchantment," and she lays "a spell" upon her oppressors. In short, she has the added boon of divinity, which empowers innocence to act.

Clearly, Clemens had no intention of presenting Joan as a typical human being. Through Le Sieur's narrative he asserts again and again that Joan is something unusual, a superhuman creature. Only through a mysterious, divine power can innocence prosper; in the world of reality and physical law its destruction is axiomatic. Clemens' deterministic ideas are largely biological and social, not metaphysical. Man, he avers, is trapped by traditions, institutions, bad blood, faulty training, and limited environment. Joan, on the other hand, transcends these restricting forces and exercises her "natural"—that is, spiritual—powers. In his essay on Joan of Arc, he asserts his belief in natural genius but claims that such a gift needs a nurturing environment. "Broadly speaking," he says, "genius is not

114

born with sight, but blind; and it is not itself that opens its eyes, but the subtle influences of a myriad of stimulating exterior circumstances." [20] Joan, however, is a marvel without peer in human history, for although she "lived in a dull little village on the frontiers of civilization," she was able to achieve greatness without external help. Le Sieur makes this same observation:

> Yes, Joan of Arc was great always, great everywhere, but she was greatest at the Rouen trials. There she rose above the limitations and infirmities of our human nature, and accomplished under blighting and unnerving and hopeless conditions all that her splended equipment of moral and intellectual forces could have accomplished if they had been supplemented by the mighty helps of hope and cheer and light, the presence of friendly faces, and a fair and equal fight, with the great world looking on and wondering. [21]

Several characters in the novel recognize this wonderful power of hers. La Hire, for example, attributes Joan's success as a general to her refusal to be tied to tradition. He notices her ability to alter with the changing circumstances of a situation instead of getting bogged down in conventional attitudes. Le Sieur calls her gift "the seeing eye" and explains, "The common eye sees only the outside of things and judges by that, but the seeing eye pierces through and reads the heart and the soul, finding there capacities which the outside didn't indicate or promise, and which the other kind of eye couldn't detect." [22] This is not the first appearance of this gift in Clemens' work, although it may be the first explicit statement of it. The "seeing eye" seems to define that detached view which Clemens' innocents have when they remove themselves from society. It is the Greenhorn's ability to perceive the folly of social institutions, Captain Stormfield's capacity for judging Negroes and Jews correctly in heaven, and Huck's skeptical insight into civilized hypocrisy. It is, in short, the intuitive perception natural to every innocent by virtue of his good heart. Its particular importance in *Joan of Arc* derives from its being mystically, rather than naturalistically, inspired.

Clemens combines these several traits—innocence, anti-institutionalism, natural divinity, and regenerative power—with Joan's historical mission—the salvation of her people—to make her a very special kind of patriot. In the first place, although she attends mass and professes allegiance to her religion, she appears to be a Protestant.

She receives her strength and inspiration directly from God, not through the Church. The ecclesiastical courts very properly condemn her claims of divine communication, I should think, for these place her in league with such heretical mystics as Amaury of Bene, whom the Church burned at the stake in the thirteenth century for similar views. As an innocent she is without original sin, "without spot or stain of baseness." In her examination by the doctors at Poitiers she cites the Bible as her supreme authority and denies the validity of the Patrologies. All the inquisitors try to make her admit that she is confident of salvation, for the Church maintains that one cannot know that he is in a state of grace. Although Joan skillfully dodges this trap, she admits, "I have great joy in seeing [St. Michael], for when I see him I have the feeling that I am not in mortal sin."[23] Also, she places her confidence, not in Christ, the redeemer whose sacrifice is celebrated in the mass, but in God himself, whose greatest attribute is his "good heart." By virtue of her own innocent compassion she partakes in the nature of God and is not separated from him by sin. Embracing the entire benign cosmos which constitutes the innocent's world-view, she even defends the Devil. Clearly, Joan is a heretic, and the Church has good cause to execute her. But because she is a heretic, Clemens sides with her against the Church of Rome.

The second element of her patriotism is her sense of democracy. She sets out to free her people from English bondage, to drive the foreigners out of her country; and even though history demanded that she support the King of France in the novel, Clemens describes her allegiance as a populist sentiment. Le Sieur explains this idea as he comments on Joan's awareness that Charles should be crowned:

> How did she know it? It is simple: she was a peasant. That tells the whole story. She was the people and knew the people; these others moved in a loftier sphere and knew nothing much about them. We make little account of that vague, formless inert mass, that mighty underlying force which we call "the people"—an epithet which carries contempt with it. It is a strange attitude; for at bottom we know that the throne which the people support stands, and that when that support is removed nothing in this world can save it.[24]

By a transparent piece of logical manipulation Clemens has changed monarchical France into democratic France. Later, Le Sieur expresses Joan's democratic instincts in a tone of light irony, to chastize institutionalized class systems. He is ostensibly surprised to see that peasants have feelings just like the higher orders, and says, "I believe that someday it will be found out that peasants are people. Yes, beings in a great many respects like ourselves. And I believe that someday *they* will find this out too—and then! Well, then I think they will rise up and demand to be regarded as part of the race, and that by consequence there will be trouble." [25] Joan's feelings for the masses not only guide her actions, then, but they prophesy the coming revolt of the people against arbitrary authority.

As a democratic Protestant Joan advocates a doctrine of work, and Clemens contrasts her healthy vigor to the lethargy of the nobility and the corrupt intellectualism of the Church. She fights continually against the torpid aristocrats who try to impede her campaign. When she cries, "Work! work! and God will work with us," Le Sieur says, "Yes, one might say that her motto was 'Work! stick to it; keep on working!' for in war she never knew what indolence was. And whoever will take that motto and live by it will be likely to succeed." [26] Combining the strength of God with the natural energy of youth, Joan works to institute popular reforms in a land that is chained by effete traditions and constraining institutions.

These differences between Joan and her adversaries seem to place Clemens in the school of such nineteenth-century American historians as Motley and Parkman, whose work he knew and admired. These men interpreted certain historical events as a struggle between democratic, Protestant vigor and aristocratic, Catholic inertia. [27] Using this historiographical method, they portrayed past events as part of a plan of inexorable progress, which culminates in the American democratic experiment. This same interpretation of history appears in American letters; for example, in Timothy Dwight's *The Conquest of Canaan*, in which Joshua receives a vision of America, the promised land. The significance of Clemens' relationship to this particular method of viewing history is that Joan—like Dwight's Joshua and Motley's William the Silent—is a prototypical American patriot, embodying in the fifteenth century the ideal traits of the American character.

Clemens, then, seems to have solved the problems of innocence by giving it divine status. Because Joan has the power to act, she can satisfactorily represent the innocent, natural, democratic American in whom Clemens apparently wanted to believe. There is no indication of sympathy for traditional forms of government in *Joan of Arc,* as there is in *The American Claimant, Pudd'nhead Wilson,* and *A Connecticut Yankee.* These works substitute the values of a stable tradition for a kind of innocence which is too ineffectual and vulnerable to provide a basis for meaningful action. But Joan represents natural goodness raised to superhuman heights. Innocence as a mystique is not subject to destruction by real evil, so Clemens can once again place his faith in the innocent ideal. Nor does Joan inculcate the commercial, technological kind of progress that makes a villain of Hank Morgan. Instead she advocates political and religious freedom, which release man's instinctive nobility.

This survey indicates clearly the interest which Joan's story must have held for Clemens. He seems to have seen in her history those details which supported his obsessive desire to believe in man's innocence. It is not difficult to conceive of his having been immediately attracted to her because she was a child-hero who awed the world by her great capacities and influence. As a solitary figure who suffers at the hands of institutionalized society, she conforms to the pattern he has developed through all the works I have discussed so far. Her patriotic, egalitarian sympathies and her latent Protestantism fit her into a historical view that he shared with men he admired. Her success in raising herself above the strangling environment of her village home obviously appealed to his reluctant belief in environmental determinism. And most of all, her divine inspiration provided a means of overcoming the weakness from which innocence suffers in all of his works from *The Gilded Age* on.

I have not discussed *Joan of Arc* here for its literary merit. It is unashamedly sentimental, and one sees Clemens indulging his personal sorrows on every page. Nor have I included the novel because it satisfactorily solves the problem which Clemens' world-view raises. His conviction that innocence and evil are completely separate and irreconcilable has not changed, so far as I can see. Innocence still has no place in the world, for as he repeatedly maintains, Joan was like no other human being in history. Although born innocent, man is destined to succumb to social evil. If he were divine, like Joan, he could retain his goodness and act upon it; but, like Le Sieur, man is mortal, and his innocence can only bow to external corruption and restraint. Clemens' dualism continues unaltered, and although he alleviates momentarily in *Joan of Arc* the pains which this view creates, the alleviation is finally meaningless in terms of human action in a real world.

I have dealt with *Joan of Arc,* rather, because of the light it sheds on Clemens' evolving ideas. He had been working all along to find a place for innocence in his fictional world, to define the meaning of good and evil so that he might arrive at some secure point from which to see and judge reality. His treatment of the theme in this novel indicates clearly that his earlier works attempt to make innocence that foundation. His reliance on the supernatural to empower action in *Joan of Arc* suggests very strongly that he would believe in an innocent world no matter how often his own experiences violated that belief.

8.

The Angel

THE MYSTERIOUS STRANGER

BY THE TIME Clemens came to write *The Mysterious Stranger* his view of good and evil had become rigidly Manicheistic. Even in the earlier works, good and evil are irreconcilable; although innocence does exist as a state of mind, it is powerless to act in a predominantly evil world. In each successive work prior to *The Mysterious Stranger,* innocence becomes increasingly subject to evil influence, maintaining itself at first by avoiding evil, and later by operating as a mystique that is immune to worldly degeneration. Clemens seems to have had no desire to alter his opinions on the nature of innocence, but preferred to cling to his faith in natural goodness with obsessive tenacity, working out various scenes to apply the theory he held so dear. Furthermore, his Manicheism makes evil the property of the material and rational world, and relegates innocence to the realm of the spirit, the intuition, faith, and the dream. When Satan says, ''No sane man can be happy, for to him life is real and he sees what a fearful thing it is,'' [1] he explains why Clemens desired to create a world of innocent fancy in his fiction. The ideal could prosper there even though it had no place in the real world. But Satan's statement also poses a question which assumes greater urgency with each work after *Huckleberry Finn:* Of what possible use is such an idea, which obviously has no connection with reality?

The Mysterious Stranger offers no satisfactory solution to this problem. Instead it establishes one more fanciful situation in which innocence can be exonerated from the charges of impotence and irrelevance to the human situation. As in *Joan of Arc,* Clemens rearranges the real world to provide a place for his private ideal instead of examining that real world for a new and more workable theory. In this instance he advances determinism and solipsism as explanations for the failure of his ideal, but neither is convincing. In fact, both are shot through with inconsistencies which betray his real purpose in formulating them: to escape the, to him, hopeless job of revising the ideal and explaining the real world in its own terms. Like the ending of *Huckleberry Finn,* both systems betray a "failure of nerve," a refusal to admit that man's conduct does not justify the idea of innocence. His deterministic scheme attempts to turn man into a machine, but the theory bears evidence that he hung on to his belief in free, natural innocence as he constructed his philosophy. Similarly, by means of the solipsistic legerdemain in the final chapter he reverses the fanciful and real worlds, making evil a dream and innocence real. However, this scheme necessarily denies the determinism he sets up so laboriously, and contradicts many of the ideas which precede it in the story. Both systems, therefore, attack the problem from the same direction. They attempt to alter reality instead of adjusting the ideal to it. Satan's words quoted above seem to explain Clemens' shortsightedness; his notions of innocence gave him some hope, while the "insane" facts of man's existence promised him only despair.

The Mysterious Stranger involves the related careers of two innocents, Satan and Theodor Fischer. Satan is innocent because he is amoral, Theodor because he is ignorant. One can also argue that a single innocent consciousness develops as the story unfolds, in which case Theodor is the central character and Satan represents the new dimensions which his consciousness attains as he moves from ignorance to amorality. However one wants to view this matter, the two characters remain distinct until the last pages of the story, when Theodor becomes sufficiently enlightened to subsume Satan's personality; Satan embodies the ideal toward which Theodor moves as his awareness expands.

Satan explains to Theodor that he and his relatives, save his uncle, are "ignorant of sin." "We are not able to commit it," he continues, "we are without blemish, and shall abide in this state always." [2] His uncle fell because he "ate the fruit of the tree"; that is, he became aware of evil which was foreign to his nature. Satan, then, represents a new kind of innocence in Clemens' fiction; instead of being good, he is outside all moral concerns. He tells Theodor that because he has no moral sense he is above man, who does wrong because he knows what it is. For Satan no act is sinful, and so he murders the little people he has created to amuse his friends, promotes war, corrupts Ursula with money, and tells lies. But he cannot be blamed for these acts, for as Theodor ironically says, "He was only an angel and did not know any better."[3]

Satan bears many significant resemblances to the innocent heroes of Clemens' previous works. Like Huck, Tom, and Laura, he is an orphan. He is close to nature, as are Huck and Joan, and he generally appears to the boys in the woods outside town. Also, he talks to animals and sides with them against human beings. Because he is supernatural, he resembles Joan most of all. He has her beauty and her musical voice, traits which signify his great soul, just as Joan's comeliness reveals hers. Theodor notices that Satan "was a fresh breeze to the weak and the sick, whenever he came"; so he has the Maid's regenerative power. He displays this life-giving capability again when he inhabits Wilhelm's body, making his spirit shine out of the young lawyer's eyes and acting upon him like an inspiration. Once the boys have met Satan, they depend upon him for help and moral sustenance, as Joan's followers rely on her. Whenever difficulties arise Theodor exclaims, "If Satan would only come." He even carries some of Joan's qualities farther into the realm of the supernatural. Satan, too, has the "seeing eye," but it is more powerful than hers. "Nothing can obstruct my vision," he says:

> The rocks are transparent to me and darkness is daylight. I do not need an open book, I take the whole of its contents at a single glance, through the cover; and in a million years I could not forget a word of it, or its place in the volume. Nothing goes on in the skull of man, bird, fish, insect, or other creature which can be hidden from me. I pierce the learned man's brain with a single glance, and the treasures which cost him threescore years to accumulate are mine; he can forget and does forget, but I retain.[4]

He exceeds Joan, too, in being completely above human limitations. He remarks to Theodor, "I am not limited like you. I am not subject to human conditions. I can measure and understand your human weaknesses, for I have studied them, but I have none of them.''[5] He masters time and distance, which he calls ''human inventions'' and ''artificialities.'' And while Joan was divinely inspired, Satan seems actually to be God. When Nikolaus' mother says she has prayed to God to save her son, Theodor muses, ''Why He *had* saved [him]''; but Theodor is clearly referring to Satan.

Both Satan and Joan are emancipators. Joan frees her people from English bondage; Satan releases Theodor from the grip of the moral sense, man's most confining faculty. His initial feats of magic prefigure his later efforts. He makes birds and sets them free, singing, just as he eventually liberates Theodor from his mortal state at the end of the book. Clearly, Satan is virtually an extension of Joan. He is the divine innocent who can act because he is not subject to human weakness and because he can easily overcome the obstacles which evil sets in his path. When the Astrologer threatens to spoil his magic, he simply sends the old man off to the dark side of the moon. When a cruel Portuguese strikes him during his travels around the world, he casts a spell on the man and consigns him to a life of terror. Had Huck, Tom, and Laura possessed such powers, their innocence need never have been in danger.

Until Satan propels him into the empyrean in the final chapter, Theodor behaves much as Huck does when he is living at the Widow's—at least insofar as they are both good-hearted youngsters whose natural compassion is restricted only by their environments. He has a kind word for Wilhelm when it costs him nothing. He stays away from Marget, who has fallen into public disfavor, because his parents forbid him to see her. When the townspeople plot against Marget and Ursula, he says, ''We boys wanted to warn them but we backed down when it came to the pinch, being afraid. We found that we were not manly enough or brave enough to do a generous action when there was a chance that it could get us into trouble.''[6] Later, when a mob executes a suspected witch, he describes his reactions to the event: ''They hanged the lady and I threw a stone at her, although in my heart I was sorry for her, but all were throwing stones and each was watching his neighbor, and if I had not done as the others did it would have been noticed and spoken of.''[7] But prior to another lynching he is unwatched, and so he gives the victim an apple.

His good-heartedness, chained as it is, and his youthful ignorance signify his innocence. He lives in a dreamy little village near a winding river, "where news from the world hardly ever [comes] to disturb its dreams." Eseldorf is a "paradise" for boys, mainly because it lies in the bosom of a pastoral countryside, relating it to St. Petersburg, Camelot, and Domremy. In addition, his life is secure, for he lives in "the Age of Belief." He is undoubtedly ignorant, in the terms of the story, but his lack of knowledge makes happiness possible.

Dominated by social institutions, but desiring instinctively to do what is right, Theodor represents the human situation. He does not perform as a solitary innocent in rebellion against society; he symbolizes, rather, natural man in civilization. His adventures assume an allegorical significance as he moves toward cosmic innocence and away from the human attributes which prevent him from being actively good. He is Everyman struggling for perfection, and he achieves this state only by completely divorcing himself from his human limitations.

This highly simplified allegorical view leads Clemens into certain serious inconsistencies as he describes reality. For example, as the representative of his race, Theodor must show that man is a slave to social systems. Consequently, there must also be characters in the story who symbolize these institutions. Father Adolf is a witch-hunting, doctrinaire priest, Ursula a greedy self-seeker, and the Astrologer a charlatan who preys on the people's gullibility and superstition; Mueller, Klein, and Pfeiffer portray the irrational cruelty of the mob. All these characters are completely bad, as they must be to represent evil social forces. But how did man, with his naturally endowed innocence, ever create such things as "monarchies, aristocracies, and religions" to enslave and degrade himself? Throughout the novel Clemens depicts man as alternately good and bad, whichever seems to suit his polemical purpose at the moment. The little people whom Satan forms show natural pity for each other; but Marget's friends desert her when she is in trouble, return when she receives her mysterious wealth, then leave again when her father is accused of stealing the Astrologer's money. As a slave to anachronistic capitalism, man is pitiable; Wilhelm, by sticking to Marget, proves that some men can bear public censure in order to do right; and Mrs. Seppi's friends commiserate with her over her son's death. But no one will intercede for the poor widow whose dead daughter the carpenter is holding for loan collateral, and the mob at Frau Brandt's execution is incredibly cruel. There is no longer even a clear distinction between the good individual and the bad group. The action supplies no stable standards for moral judgments.

The determinism Satan preaches is, I gather, Clemens' attempt to explain how people can be malicious even though blessed with native innocence. Briefly, he argues that man is determined, first, by his moral sense and, second, by the inexorable causal connection between his acts. Because man lives by a moral code, he is capable of doing wrong. Because he lives in a universe governed by physical law, each of his acts necessarily begets the next, so that his first act as a child determines his last. Satan's two solutions to this undesirable state of affairs are, one, to remove the moral scale by which acts are judged: "There shouldn't be any wrong; and without the moral sense there couldn't be any"; [8] and, two, to juggle the sequence of man's actions by divine intercession, as he does in Nikolaus' case. In short, he remedies the difficulties of man's life by simply removing the contingencies under which that life operates.

Within these contingencies, however, there is no determinism. Man is free to choose among alternatives. Satan says, "He is always choosing, and in nine cases out of ten he prefers the wrong." [9] And even though Satan puts the act of choosing in the chain of self-determining events, choice remains open to every man within certain undeniable limits. The pattern of cause and effect which Satan outlines is nothing but a *post-facto* observation that what has happened may bear a relationship to what went before. The determinism he preaches is simply the result of his completely detached view of the matter. Within the given moral and physical system, man is free to choose and to act—even to alter the moral values according to his experience. Determinism for Clemens is the collected facts of life.

These facts merely limit man's ability to be Satan; they do not control his destiny. Furthermore, they do not explain why man behaves badly when he is supposedly born good.

"Man is a prisoner for life," Theodor laments; and Satan answers, "But I can free him." This is his purpose in the novel. Through the course of his interviews with Theodor he slowly weans the boy away from his human participation in life and gives him a disinterested, comic, detached view of existence. He begins by impressing Theodor with man's pettiness in the cosmic scheme and giving him some vague idea of the extent of time and space outside the mortal world. He instructs the boy by analogizing the difference between himself and a human being. During this period of training he repeatedly admonishes his pupil to "stand off a piece, out of danger" and look at reality from outside the moral and physical laws which give the world its recognizable form. He shows Theodor the human race by fashioning dolls out of clay, by making him invisible, by suspending him high over China, and by passing a phantom pageant before his eyes. In each of these visions Theodor remains aloof, uninvolved. He learns to see life "theoretically," as Satan does, not experientially, which the boy himself admits is the "only way."

While training Theodor to see the world from his own lofty vantage point, Satan also gives him periodic mystical intimations of heaven. At their first meeting he plays upon his flute, and Theodor exclaims, "There is no music like that, unless perhaps in heaven, and that was where he brought it from." The enraptured boy then describes the merrymaking that follows: "It made one mad, for pleasure; and we could not take our eyes from him, and the looks that went out of our eyes came from our hearts and their dumb speech was worship. He brought the dance from heaven, too, and the bliss of paradise was in it." Each time Satan reappears, a wonderful euphoria comes over Theodor; and after showing his young protégé the horrors of civilization, Satan gives him wine which evokes in him a sense of paradise. As they drink, Satan offers a significant toast: "We will drink to one another's health and let civilization go." [10]

By means of these lessons, Satan teaches Theodor to view life as an imprisonment and death as release. As the boy watches a lynch-mob fighting among themselves, he notices "the dead lady hanging from her rope, her troubles forgotten, her spirit at peace." Moreover, Satan advocates the comic view of life appropriate to the detachment he provides. "Power, money, persuasion, supplication," he says, "can lift at a colossal humbug . . . but only laughter can blow it to rags and atoms at a blast." [11] Everything is hopeless; God is in "shattered health"; faith is no longer a protection against evil and despair; "There is nowhere to look for help." The only solace lies in escape from life into cosmic innocence.

Viewed in this context, the final chapter appears to be the logical conclusion to the events which precede it in the novel. Once the moral sense is removed there is no longer any need for heaven and hell, since all actions have equal moral value. Furthermore, when one looks at the world with sufficient detachment it assumes a purely theoretical significance, and one can dismiss it by rejecting the theory which one has formulated. Reality taken as pure thought has only the most fragile substance when one is as suspicious of abstract thought as Clemens seems to have been. As Theodor concludes, the thought which remains is "a vagrant thought, a useless thought, a homeless thought wandering forlorn among empty eternities." Having first rejected the mind as a satisfactory guide to action in his deterministic philosophy, Clemens now abandons reality. This is more than solipsism, obviously; it is pure nihilism. But at least it affords escape from the "frankly and hysterically insane" conditions in which Clemens found himself.

The ending seems symbolically justified also. In his first description of Eseldorf, Theodore says that the village is "asleep" and that no knowledge of the outside world disturbs its dreams. Even the name—"assville"—implies that Clemens does not see the village as the last resort of innocence. It signifies, mainly, ignorance in its pejorative sense; so he can justifiably annihilate it when Theodor becomes enlightened. Also, Clemens continually insists that enchantment is real, in order to break down the barriers between the material and dream worlds. After watching Satan perform a miracle, Theodor says, "It seemed almost too good to be true, that we were actually seeing these romantic and wonderful things, and that it was not a dream." [12] When Father Adolf fails to turn the miraculous food to ashes through exorcism, Theodor realizes that Satan's magic is genuine. Even the blood that gushes from Jael's phantom guest as she drives a nail into his temple is real, for Theodor says, "We could have stained our hands in it if we had wanted to." Clemens may have intended these equivocations to prepare for the final reversal of reality and fancy—his method of dealing with evil in the novel. Much of Clemens' later unpublished material deals with the confusion of the dream and waking states, and having consistently portrayed the Innocent Land as a dream world in his earlier novels, he needed only to apply the same confusion to *The Mysterious Stranger* to make cosmic innocence real, and evil a nightmare.

On the other hand, there is considerable evidence that Clemens did not have this ending in mind when he wrote the greatest part of the story. In the first place, Albert Bigelow Paine discovered the manuscript unfinished among Clemens' papers. He also found several conclusions and selected the one which appears in published versions of the novel. Furthermore, the narrator seems to be a disillusioned old man, somewhat like the speaker in *Roughing It* and Le Sieur in *Joan of Arc*. As he begins the story he says, "I was only a boy," suggesting that at the time he is speaking he is an adult, not a vagrant thought. Also, there are examples of his later opinions sprinkled throughout the narrative, which imply that an adult consciousness has developed out of the action. For example, he says that the townspeople's idea that Father Peter's money came from the Devil is a good guess for "ignorant people like that." This is not the boy's attitude, for he is as unenlightened as they. Then, Theodor's remarks on his last days with Nikolaus are not those of a boy who has left the world as an adolescent. He says, "In effect they were days of companionship with one's sacred dead and I have known no comradeship that was so close or so precious." [13] These are clearly the words of an old man looking back over a long career of acquaintances and sorrows. I grant that it might be difficult to create a narrative voice out of a disembodied thought, but that is not what Clemens seems to have had in mind as he told the story. There is little reason to believe that he would devote over one hundred pages to a methodical castigation of social evil, planning all the while to pass it off as a bad dream in the last few paragraphs.

I adduce this evidence to suggest that Clemens did not know how to end his novel; simply his failure to finish it strongly supports this notion. Paine's choice of a conclusion attests to his critical acumen (not particularly noticeable elsewhere); for the chapter he selected is the only one possible.[14] The almost totally pessimistic tenor of the story, with its lack of any foundations for either a tragic outcome or a satisfactory philosophic reconciliation, demands that it end on a note of evasion. Like *Huckleberry Finn, The Mysterious Stranger* sets up an insoluble problem: innocence exists, but there is no place for it in man's necessarily corrupt situation. Consequently, the conclusions of both works are essentially the same. They admit by their disregard for the stated problem that the dichotomy of good and evil cannot be resolved, and that the dilemma can best be settled with a gimmick.

Earlier I stated that Clemens' deterministic philosophy contains suggestions of his basic disbelief in that he erected it mainly in order to justify what he considered man's inability to do good. I believe also that his ideas, as he outlined them in his essay, *What is Man?*, illuminate the central moral problem of his major fictions, and that they explain why determinism received its first explicit statement at the same time that he relegated innocence entirely to the realm of the supernatural.

What is Man? sets forth in greater detail essentially the same ideas which Satan outlines in *The Mysterious Stranger*. Those minor inconsistencies which appear between the two statements I take to be faults of the system itself, rather than deliberate alterations of its fundamental propositions. To begin, Clemens' philosophy is naturalistic, not spiritual. Heredity, environment, and training make up man's nature: "Whatsoever a man is, is due to his *make* . . . his heredities, his habitat, his associations."[15] For this reason, Satan in the novel usually concentrates on describing man in his worldly state and diagnosing his characteristics as effects of that state. Second, the system is generally psychological, since it explains man's nature according to the various faculties of his mind; and it is specifically behavioristic, since man's actions evidence these faculties while the mind itself has no control over his actions. Satan operates on these assumptions also, for he discusses mainly what man does rather than

129

how he thinks. The deterministic character of the theory necessitates this emphasis, of course, because Clemens' primary aim is to free men from responsibility for his own deeds.

The dominant faculty in man's composition is the Interior Master. Everything man does, he does to satisfy this Master's demands. That is, man performs all deeds to satisfy himself. In different men this Master requires different kinds of satisfaction, but the end result is always the same: man's motives are entirely selfish. Also, as the Old Man of the essay says, public approval is often the surest measure of self-approval. The Interior Master, the Old Man continues, is made up of Temperament and Associations. Man is born with his Temperament, which he inherits from his ancestors' training. He cannot alter this legacy, but he can control it. For example, if he tends to be hot-tempered he can refuse to misbehave when his ire is aroused. Associations are the sum of man's experiences—his friends, his family, his reading, and so on. Man can also select these associations to some extent, and thereby guide the desires of his Interior Master. In fact, says the Old Man, that is what governments should do for their people. Temperament and Associations, then, make up the Interior Master, and within certain limits, man may control both.

The second major subdivision of man's nature is the Mind, the critical faculty which distinguishes between right and wrong. This faculty, however, has no influence on the Will (the Interior Master), which alone dictates action. Although a man may perceive the moral difference between acts, he must perform the one that will satisfy his inner longing, the one that will give him self-satisfaction. Man can train his mind also, by study, but apparently such activity is useless, since this training never bears fruit in the form of action. As Satan says, man knows the difference between right and wrong, but he generally chooses the wrong. The mind, then, is the conscience or moral sense, which Satan speaks of as being valueless. Because it only designates wrong, without facilitating a commensurate course of action, it merely creates anxiety and senseless guilt.

This system, even without the several side issues explored in the essay, embraces some serious inconsistencies. In the first place, the doctrine of self-approval is in no wise deterministic. Temperament and Associations, which comprise the Interior Master, can and should be trained so that man will desire good instead of evil. The Old Man says, "Diligently train your ideals *upward* and *still upward* toward a summit where you will find your chiefest pleasure in conduct which, while contenting you, will be surest to confer benefits upon your neighbor and the community." [16] This gospel, he admits, has been taught by "all the great religions." But what is that summit really? How can man perceive it if his main desire is self-satisfaction? If he is not free, why is one direction on the mountain any more desirable than another? Also, if he has no will, what need has he of admonitions of this kind; he cannot act upon them.

By "summit" the Old Man seems to mean a kind of general good, brotherly love, compassion—the qualities which I have designated as comprising natural innocence. Since the mind has no effect on the will, and since the will concerns itself with self-satisfaction, this urge to seek the summit must enter man's being through some other portal. Clemens implies the answer to this problem as he defines the limitations of Temperament and Association. The Young Man asks if he will ever be able to behave nobly, and the Old Man answers, "Why—yes. In heaven," where the restrictions of heredity and environment disappear. Apparently these limiting factors curb only man's natural tendency toward good. They do not restrict any evil potential; in fact, they cause it. Man possesses a will to do good which cannot function so long as he remains oppressed by bad blood and corrupt society. Once again, despite his philosophical skullduggery, Clemens comes back to his old notion of good man made bad by his worldly situation.

This whole problem, it seems, resolves itself into a conflict between the ideal (innocence) and the real (evil). Determinism is simply another name for reality, and the only seriously limiting forces which exist are man's worldly circumstances. Even these, as Clemens admits, are alterable in accordance with the ideal; but so long as man remains a human being he can never achieve the ideal which Clemens sets up for him.

Fundamentally, these ideas are the stuff of tragedy. A man of great mental powers perceives the gulf between what is and what ought to be. He then either makes a noble effort to impose the ideal on reality, bringing his world down about him as he experiences enlightening defeat; or he makes a compromise, adjusting his actions to the requirements of reality and accepting the margin as personal tragedy. In neither case does he ignore reality, excuse it as meaningless, and adhere to an ideal that is completely at odds with reality. If he recognizes the absurd impracticality of his ideal and still pursues it, he is a fanatic. If he does not have the mental acumen to see the necessary imperfections and compromises of reality, he is a victim. Both of these types may become tragic heroes, but only through enlightenment. As long as they retain their narrow vision, they miss the requirements of tragedy.

Similarly, these ideas can be turned to comic effects. Men of common sense deride the fanatic and bring him back to reality; or the victim, in making his compromise with life, comments sardonically on both the impractical ideal and the imperfect world. But however the artist sees the situation, it must lead to a reconciliation of some kind. Somewhere along the line the mind must realize the meaning of the action in which it is involved. The hero must learn to guide future action—even if none is vouchsafed him because he perishes—according to his enlightened view. Furthermore, this future action must take place in the real world, for the ostensible purpose of literary art is to give the human mind the means to live significantly in the world. Art appears meretricious when it insists that man cannot exist in his native situation and that his only hope is to escape.

In his philosophy Clemens seems to have discounted the one faculty that can recognize the ideal, the real, and the necessary compromises which must be made between them. The mind, he says, is the critical sense which evaluates experience and decides what is right and wrong. But the mind is powerless to guide human action; it has no influence over the will. Believing this, he must conclude that no amount of experience can ever enable man to determine his own fate, even within certain fixed limits. The mind can only perceive the corruption and constraint which restrict natural goodness; it cannot do anything about them. In fact, the mind itself destroys man's innocence, for it brings him "news from the outside world," and that news is all bad.

Clemens cut himself off from the possibility of attaining either a comic or tragic resolution in *The Mysterious Stranger* by relegating the mind to a position of incapacity. In place of the mind as the source and test of rightness, he posits a powerful but ineffable and ultimately undefinable personal sense; and he objectifies this personal sense as natural goodness—innocence. Then, because he finds neither evidence nor purpose for innocence in the world as he sees it, he elevates innocence to the status of a mystique and turns reality, first, into a machine, and then into a dream. As long as natural goodness could maintain itself in the world, either by evasion or divine inspiration, he seems to have been willing to bear the human condition—if only on the level of pathos or sentiment. But in *The Mysterious Stranger* he has apparently abandoned hope in reality altogether. He adheres more tenaciously than ever to his ideal, but there is no reconciliation with reality. The river and the village by the flowery meadow are not far enough away from the world in *The Mysterious Stranger*. Theodor must escape his human body, since it too is an evil machine; so Clemens launches his hero's consciousness, first, into amoral heaven, and finally into limitless space.

The Mysterious Stranger thus marks the logical conclusion to the trend I have been describing all along. Even in the early works, innocence could not survive in civilization. Urban settings smother natural goodness with their conventions and institutions. Only in nature can innocence display itself in the form of brotherhood, general good will, repose, and native sagacity. In each successive work evil grows in power and extent, driving innocence farther off in search of safety. It escapes to ante-bellum Hannibal, but society is there to threaten it. It flees back in time to Arthurian England, but the seducer follows and destroys it. It receives divine aid, but evil still eradicates its mortal form. Finally, it vanishes into the infinite cosmos, where it wanders alone, free at last, but useless.

Clemens' original conception, that evil and goodness are absolutely irreconcilable, does not seem to change substantially between *The Innocents Abroad* and *The Mysterious Stranger*. The difference in his treatment of innocence in the various books is due, I believe, to his growing conviction that evil predominates in the real world. As he grew older he seems to have found less and less justification for his ideal of natural goodness in the life that went on about him; but he could not compromise this ideal, for reality offered him nothing that could compensate for its loss. Had he been able to alter his dream of innocence as his perception of human weakness deepened, and to reconcile his desires with reality, his fiction might have gotten progressively better, instead of culminating with the definitive statement of the problem in *Huckleberry Finn.* But he apparently could not bring himself to dilute his faith in innocence. The cynical, disillusioned philosopher of *What is Man?* seems to speak for Clemens when he says, ''Having found the Truth . . . the rest of my days will be spent in patching and painting and puttying and caulking my priceless possession and in looking the other way when an imploring argument or a damaging fact approaches.'' [17]

Notes to the Text

Chapter One

[1] " . . . the proposition, implicit in much American writing from Poe and Cooper to Anderson and Hemingway, that the valid rite of initiation for the individual in the new world is not an initiation *into* society, but, given the character of society, an initiation *away from it:* something I wish it were legitimate to call *'denitiation.'* " R. W. B. Lewis, *The American Adam* (Chicago: University of Chicago Press), p. 115.

[2] See also Kenneth Lynn, *Mark Twain and Southwestern Humor* (Boston and Toronto: Little, Brown and Co., 1959), pp. 64-72.

[3] *Ibid.,* p. 146.

[4] S. L. Clemens, *The Definitive Edition of the Collected Writings of Mark Twain,* ed. Albert Bigelow Paine, 35 vols. (New York: Gabriel Wells, 1922-25), VII, 18 (hereafter referred to as *Works*).

[5] See also Kenneth Lynn, *op. cit.,* pp. 17-18.

[6] See Franklin Rogers, *Mark Twain's Burlesque Patterns as Seen in the Novels and Narratives, 1855-1885* (Dallas: Southern Methodist University Press, 1960), *passim.*

[7] S. L. Clemens, *Mark Twain's Travels with Mr. Brown,* eds. Franklin Walker and G. Ezra Dane (New York: A. A. Knopf, 1940), p. 41.

[8] *Works,* I, 11.

[9] *Ibid.,* p. 64.

[10] *Works,* II, 302.

[11] *Ibid.,* p. 345.

[12] *Ibid.,* pp. 330-31.

[13] *Works,* I, 17.

[14] R. W. B. Lewis, *op. cit.,* pp. 91-92.

[15] *Works,* I, 241.

Chapter Two

[1] Clemens prepared the earliest draft of "Captain Stormfield" now extant in 1873. Although he revised the story many times between that date and 1907, when he finally published it, that early version contains the structure and the vernacular narrative which are important here. See Dixon Wecter's introduction to *Report from Paradise,* by S. L. Clemens (New York: Harper and Bros., 1952), p. xxii.

[2] *Works,* III, 5.

[3] *Ibid.,* p. 7.

[4] *Ibid.,* p. 93.

[5] *Works,* IV, 5.

[6] *Ibid.,* p. 130.

[7] *Ibid.,* pp. 131-32.

[8] *Ibid.,* pp. 177, 179.

[9] *Ibid.,* pp. 186, 188.

[10] *Ibid.,* pp. 202, 208, 211.

[11] *Ibid.,* p. 266.

[12] *Ibid.,* p. 283.

[13] S. L. Clemens, *Report from Paradise,* pp. 1-2.

[14] Dixon Wecter says, "No portion of the Stormfield cycle invokes the presence of God, although an unpublished fragment refers with elaborate circumlocution to 'the authorities.'" (*Report from Paradise,* p. xviii.) The relationship implied here between guide-books, the Bible, and God is clear. All are "authorities" which blind men to reality and which he must cast off as he undergoes education.

[15] *Report from Paradise,* pp. 7-8.

[16] *Ibid.,* p. 13.

Chapter Three

[1] Kenneth Lynn, *Mark Twain and Southwestern Humor,* p. 177.

[2] Quoted in Dixon Wecter, *Sam Clemens of Hannibal* (Boston: Houghton Mifflin Co., 1952), p. 219.

[3] *Ibid.,* pp. 177-78.

[4] S. L. Clemens, *Mark Twain in Eruption,* ed. Bernard DeVoto (New York: Harper & Bros., 1940), p. 77.

[5] *Works,* V, 27-28.

[6] *Ibid.,* p. 51.

[7] *Ibid.,* pp. 64-65.

[8] *Ibid.,* p. 98.

[9] *Ibid.,* p. 102.

[10] For the division of chapters between Clemens and Warner, see Albert Bigelow Paine, *Mark Twain: A Biography,* 3 vols. (New York: Harper & Bros., 1912), I, 477.

[11] S. L. Clemens, *Letters from the Earth,* ed. Bernard DeVoto (New York: Harper and Row, 1962), pp. 8, 16-21, 37-42.

[12] *Works,* V, 186.

[13] *Ibid.,* p. 192.

[14] *Ibid.,* p. 132.

[15] *Ibid.,* p. 240.

[16] *Ibid.,* p. 253.

[17] *Ibid.,* p. 299.

[18] See Walter Blair, *Mark Twain and Huck Finn* (Berkeley: University of California Press, 1960), pp. 64-66.

[19] H. N. Smith and W. M. Gibson, eds., *The Mark Twain–Howells Letters: The Correspondence of Samuel L. Clemens and William D. Howells, 1872-1910,* 2 vols. (Cambridge, Mass.: Belknap Press of Harvard University Press, 1960), p. 91.

[20] New York *Herald,* August 17, 1890. Quoted in Svend Peterson, *Mark Twain and the Government* (Caldwell, Idaho: Caxton Printers, Ltd., 1960), p. 37.

[21] *The Mark Twain–Howells Letters,* p. 92.

[22] *Works,* VIII, 13.

[23] *Ibid.,* p. 65.

[24] *Ibid.,* p. 124.

[25] Walter Blair, *Mark Twain and Huck Finn,* pp. 55-56.

[26] *Ibid.,* pp. 66, 67.

[27] *Works,* VIII, 288.

Chapter Four

[1] See also Walter Blair, *Mark Twain and Huck Finn,* Chapter 13, for a discussion of material in *The Prince and the Pauper* which bears directly on *Huckleberry Finn.*

[2] Clemens wrote "Old Times on the Mississippi" for serial publication in *Atlantic* magazine and incorporated it later in *Life on the Mississippi,* where it appears as Chapters 4-17. Since the chapters he added to the *Atlantic* series in preparing the book furnish some information on the original material, I use *Life on the Mississippi (Works,* XII) as a reference in this chapter to simplify documentation.

[3] *Works,* XII, 36.

[4] *Ibid.,* pp. 78-80.

[5] *Works,* XI, 104-105.

[6] *Ibid.,* pp. 150-51.

[7] *Ibid.,* p. 198.

[8] *Works,* XV, 281.

[9] *Ibid.,* pp. 278-79.

[10] *Ibid.,* p. 260.

[11] *Ibid.,* p. 257.

[12] R. W. B. Lewis, *The American Adam,* p. 84.

[13] *Works,* VIII, epilogue.

[14] Commenting in 1905 on Jack Van Nostrand, one of the *Quaker City* passengers, Clemens indicated his preference for early death over adult despair: "Because he died at that early age . . . he had seen all there was to see of this world that was illusion, and illusion is the only valuable thing in it." S. L. Clemens, *Mark Twain's Speeches* (New York: Harper & Bros., 1910), p. 248.

Chapter Five

[1] Henry Nash Smith, *Mark Twain: The Development of a Writer* (Cambridge, Mass.: Belknap Press of Harvard University Press, 1962), p. 20.

[2] See also H. N. Smith, *Mark Twain,* Chapter VI.

[3] *Works,* XIII, 48-50.

[4] Walter Blair, *Mark Twain and Huck Finn,* Chapter XI.

[5] The feud between the two families—the origins of which no one in the story can remember—may well have begun as a battle between farmers (grangers) and shepherds long before in England. Since the enclosure movement had no relevance to agrarian life in the old Southwest, the feud represents a debilitating tradition carried over from the Old World.

[6] See Leo Marx, "Mr. Eliot, Mr. Trilling, and *Huckleberry Finn,*" *American Scholar,* XXII (Autumn, 1953), 433.

[7] *Works,* XIII, 162.

[8] *Ibid.,* p. 225.

[9] *Ibid.,* p. 440.

[10] The speech is reprinted in *Works,* XXVIII, 63-68.

[11] S. L. Clemens, *Mark Twain's Speeches,* pp. 17-24.

Chapter Six

[1] *Works,* XIV, 449.

[2] A. B. Paine, *Mark Twain: A Biography,* III, 1656-57.

[3] H. N. Smith and W. M. Gibson, eds., *The Mark Twain–Howells Letters,* p. 613.

[4] S. L. Clemens, *Mark Twain's Speeches,* p. 414.

[5] *Ibid.,* pp. 304 ff.

[6] S. L. Clemens, *Mark Twain's Notebook,* ed. A. B. Paine (New York: Harper & Bros., 1935), p. 395.

[7] S. L. Clemens, *Mark Twain to Mrs. Fairbanks,* ed. Dixon Wecter (San Marino, Calif.: Huntington Library, 1949), p. 208.

[8] *Works,* XIV, 237.

[9] Letter to Dan Beard, illustrator of *A Connecticut Yankee,* quoted in A. B. Paine, *Mark Twain: A Biography,* II, 888.

[10] *Works,* XIV, 45.

[11] *Ibid.,* p. 230.

[12] *Ibid.,* p. 311.

[13] *Ibid.,* p. 10.

[14] *Ibid.,* p. 22.

[15] *Ibid.,* p. 53.

[16] *Ibid.,* p. 39.

[17] *Ibid.,* p. 43.

[18] *Ibid.,* pp. 47, 48.

[19] *Ibid.,* p. 55.

[20] *Ibid.,* p. 66.

[21] *Ibid.,* p. 56.

[22] *Ibid.,* p. 22.

[23] S. L. Clemens, *Mark Twain's Notebook,* p. 367.

[24] *Works,* XIV, 93.

[25] *Ibid.,* p. 107.

[26] *Ibid.,* pp. 102-103.

[27] *Ibid.,* p. 226.

[28] *Ibid.,* p. 291.

[29] *Ibid.,* p. 301.

[30] *Ibid.,* p. 335.

[31] *Ibid.,* p. 382.

[32] *Ibid.,* p. 270.

[33] *Ibid.,* p. 386.

[34] *Ibid.,* p. 61.

Chapter Seven

[1] See also, A. E. Stone, *The Innocent Eye* (New Haven: Yale University Press, 1961), Chapter VII.

[2] *Works,* XVII, xxvii.

[3] *Ibid.,* pp. 16-17.

[4] *Ibid.,* p. 298.

[5] *Works,* XVIII, 5-6.
[6] *Ibid.,* p. 109.
[7] *Ibid.,* p. 110.
[8] *Ibid.,* p. 276.
[9] *Works,* XXII, 381.
[10] *Works,* XVII, 139.
[11] *Works,* XXII, 367.
[12] *Works,* XVIII, 108.
[13] *Ibid.,* p. 281.
[14] *Works,* XVII, 13.
[15] *Works,* XVIII, 5.
[16] *Ibid.,* p. 228.
[17] *Works,* XVII, 304.
[18] *Works,* XVIII, 123.
[19] *Works,* XVII, 161.
[20] *Works,* XXII, 377.
[21] *Works,* XVIII, 230.
[22] *Works,* XVII, 180.
[23] *Works,* XVIII, 172.
[24] *Ibid.,* p. 28.
[25] *Ibid.,* p. 65.
[26] *Works,* XVII, 302.
[27] See David Levin, *History as Romantic Art* (Stanford: Stanford University Press, 1959), *passim.*

Chapter Eight

[1] *Works,* XXVII, 130.
[2] *Ibid.,* p. 16.
[3] *Ibid.,* p. 49.
[4] *Ibid.,* p. 80.
[5] *Ibid.,* p. 23.
[6] *Ibid.,* p. 65.
[7] *Ibid.,* p. 115.
[8] *Ibid.,* p. 151.
[9] *Ibid.,* p. 52.
[10] *Ibid.,* p. 22.
[11] *Ibid.,* p. 132.
[12] *Ibid.,* p. 24.
[13] *Ibid.,* p. 94.
[14] J. S. Tuckey's study of the *Mysterious Stranger* manuscripts does not dissuade me from this opinion, however helpful it may be in reassessing

Clemens' later writings. See *Mark Twain and Little Satan* (West Lafayette, Ind.: Purdue University Press, 1963), *passim.*

[15] *Works,* XXVI, 5.

[16] *Ibid.,* pp. 54-55.

[17] *Ibid.,* p. 75.

Index

Amaury of Bene, 116
Aristotle, 58
Artemus Ward, 7

Blair, Walter, 44, 45, 74
Bowen, Mrs. Will, 39

Calvinism, x, xii, 1, 2
Clemens, Olivia Langdon, 40, 62
Clemens, Samuel L., *Works:*
  Address to Plymouth Society
    (1881), 81
  Adventures of Huckleberry Finn,
    ix, xii, xiii, xiv, 4, 5, 13, 24,
    27, 28, 30, 31, 32, 36, 42, 46,
    47, 48, 53, 55, 60, 61-83, 86,
    88, 90, 92, 93, 94, 96-97, 104,
    105, 106, 114, 115, 120, 121,
    122, 123, 124, 129, 133, 134
  The Adventures of Tom Sawyer,
    xiii, 4, 31-32, 36, 40-47, 52,
    53, 57, 59, 63, 65, 66, 67, 68,
    70, 72, 79, 89, 90, 105, 106,
    122, 123, 133
  The American Claimant, 93, 118
  "A Boy's Manuscript," 41, 44
  "Captain Stormfield's Visit to
    Heaven," 1, 3, 5, 15, 26-30,
    37, 50, 51, 52, 55, 59, 68, 69,
    72, 78, 88, 105, 115
  "The Celebrated Jumping Frog
    of Calaveras County," 5-7,
    14, 27, 68, 88

*A Connecticut Yankee in King
  Arthur's Court,* xiv, 13, 54,
  84-104, 105, 106, 118, 124,
  133
"The Dandy Frightening the
  Squatter," 6
Fulton Day Address (1907), 87
The Gilded Age, xiii, 4, 31-40,
  43, 47, 48, 52, 59, 65, 67, 79,
  105-106, 118, 122, 123
The Innocents Abroad, xiii, xiv,
  5, 8, 9-14, 15, 16, 17, 18, 27,
  28, 29, 30, 31, 37, 49, 50, 51,
  52, 55, 59, 65, 86, 89, 93, 133
Joan of Arc, xiii, xiv, 24, 36, 40,
  105-119, 121, 122-123, 124,
  128, 133
Lecture to the Stomach Club, 36
Letters from the Earth, 36
The Mysterious Stranger, xiv,
  xv, 13, 25, 55, 89, 92, 95,
  120-129, 130, 133-134
"Old Times on the Mississippi,"
  48-52, 56, 59, 65, 105, 106
The Prince and the Pauper, 13,
  48, 52-55, 59, 60, 65, 70, 99,
  105, 106
"The Private History of a
  Campaign That Failed,"
  48, 55-59, 65, 108
Pudd'nhead Wilson, 1, 36, 93,
  118

Index

Roughing It, xii, xiii, xiv, 1, 3, 4, 13, 15-26, 28, 29, 30, 37, 43, 48, 49, 50, 51, 52, 54, 55, 59, 65, 69-70, 72, 79, 86, 91, 105, 107, 115, 128

Sacramento *Union* Correspondence, 7-9, 14

San Francisco *Alta California* Correspondence, 7-9, 14

1601, 36

"Snodgrass Letters," 6, 68

"St. Joan of Arc," 111, 115

"To a Person Sitting in Darkness," 96

"Villagers of 1840-3," 33

What Is Man?, 129-134

Cooper, James F., 2, 13

Determinism, 120-134 *passim.*

Dickinson, Emily, xi, 61-62

Don Quixote, 7

Dwight, Timothy, 117

Emerson, Ralph W., 81

Enlightenment, The, x

Evangelism, 9

Fairbanks, Mrs., 87

Great Awakening, The, x

Grotius, Hugo, 2

Hawthorne, Nathaniel, xi, 61-62
    The Scarlet Letter, xiii

Hemingway, Ernest, xiii

Howells, William D., 42, 66, 85

James, Henry, 2, 4

Jefferson, Thomas, 3

Kipling, Rudyard, 42

Lewis, R. W. B., 13, 58

Locke, John, 2

Longfellow, Henry W., 81

Lynn, Kenneth, 6, 32

Manicheism, 120

"Mark Twain" (Pseudonym), 7

Marx, Leo, 79

Melville, Herman, xi, 2, 13, 61-62
    Moby-Dick, xiii, 2

Motley, John L., 117-118

Paine, Albert B., 128-129

Parkman, Francis, 13, 117

Protestantism, 116, 118

Romanticism, x, 2, 56

Rousseau, Jean J., 2

Smith, Henry N., 62

Southwestern American Humor, 4, 5, 14

Virginia City *Enterprise,* 7, 86

Warner, Charles D., 32, 35, 36, 37, 40

Whitman, Walt, 13

Whittier Birthday Dinner, 80-81

DATE DUE